PRAYER M. MADUEKE

91 days
DECREES
TO
TAKEOVER
THE YEAR

PRAYER
PUBLICATIONS
UNITED STATES

ISBN: 979-8565566949

Published by Prayer Publications.
Printed in the United States of America.

4 Free Ebooks

In order to say a 'Thank You' for purchasing *91 Days Decrees to Takeover the Year*, I offer these books to you in appreciation. Click or type madu.eke.com/free-gift in your browser.

Message from the Author

I want to see you succeed, grow, and break free from negativity and obstacles. My hope is for you to thrive, unaffected by negative influences and challenging situations. Because of that, please permit me to introduce two courses that I believe passionately will help you:

1. To break the evil altars and powers of your father's house, The role of altars in the realm of existence is very key because altars are meeting places between the physical and the spiritual, between the visible and the invisible.

    Unless a man cuts off the evil flow from the power of his father's house, he will not fulfil his destiny. Click here to learn more about my course on how to tear down unholy altars and close the enemy's entryways into your life!

2. To help you seamlessly break iron-like problems, illness, delayed marriage, poverty, or any long-standing battle.

    Discover the transformative power of Christian fasting and prayer. Remember, Matthew 17:21 teaches us, *"But this kind of demon does not go out except by prayer and fasting."* Ready to overcome your struggles? Click here to learn more about this course.

Embrace the journey ahead with faith, for through prayer, fasting, and the dismantling of evil altars, you shall unlock the doors to spiritual liberation and divine breakthrough. May your path be illuminated by His grace as you walk towards a life free from bondage.

If you're seeing this from the physical copy, type the link: madueke.com/courses in your browser to view all the courses on my website.

Prayer Madueke
CHRISTIAN AUTHOR

Christian Counselling

We were created for a greater purpose than only survival and God wants us to live a full life.

If you need prayer or counselling, or if you have any other inquiries, please visit the counselling page on my website to know when I will be available for a phone call.

Click or type **links.madueke.com/counselling** in your browser.

Let's Connect on Youtube ▶

Join me on my YouTube channel, "Prayer M. Madueke," where I share powerful insights, guidance, and prayers for spiritual breakthroughs.

Subscribe today to unlock the secrets of the Kingdom and embrace an abundant life. Let's grow together!

Click or type **links.madueke.com/youtube** in your browser.

Table of Contents

DECREE SECTION

CHAPTER ONE

CHALLENGES TO PRAY

Moses went to the mountain and prayed till God gave him a law that will guide him to rule his people. Joshua prayed and the sun and the moon stopped moving for a day. Hannah prayed and God gave her Samuel. Elijah prayed and God confirmed his ministry by fire. Jehoshaphat prayed and his stubborn enemies got confused and began to kill themselves.

The people of Nineveh prayed and God gave them mass repentance and national deliverance. Daniel prayed and God closed the mouths of the lions that were starved to eat him up. Esther prayed and the king could not sleep until the decree against God's children was reversed and their enemies avenged. Nehemiah prayed and God gave him a national assignment.

Enoch prayed and God empowered him to walk with him until the day he left this world. Jacob prayed and God changed his name and made him a great prince. Hezekiah prayed and God changed the death verdict that was against him and added fifteen more years to his year. Jabez prayed and God enlarged his coast, removed poverty from him and blessed him mightily.

The believers in Peter's day prayed and the prison doors opened and set Peter free. The wife of one of the sons of the prophet prayed and God saved her two sons and she opened an oil company. The daughters of Zelophehad asked Moses a great question. Your father has a name that must not be done away with from among his family. Are you saying that because you are not a man but a woman, your father's possession should be done away with?

The daughters of Zelophehad challenged Moses and forced him to release their father's inheritance.

'Why should the name of our father be done away from among his family, because he hath no son? Give unto us therefore a possession among the brethren of our father' (Numbers 27:4).

'And Moses brought their cause before the LORD. And the LORD spake unto Moses, saying, the daughters of Zelophehad speak right: thou shalt surely give them a possession of an inheritance among their father's brethren; and thou shalt cause the inheritance of their father to pass unto them. And thou shalt speak unto the children of Israel, saying, if a man dies, and have no son, then ye shall cause his inheritance to pass unto his daughter. And if he has no daughter, then ye shall give his inheritance unto his brethren. And if he has no brethren, then ye shall give his inheritance unto his father's brethren. And if his father has no brethren, then ye shall give his inheritance unto his kinsman that is next to him of his family, and he shall possess it: and it shall be unto the children of Israel a statute of judgment, as the LORD commanded Moses' (Number 27:5-11).

God said that the daughters of Zelophehad were right. Esther went on hunger strike, a suicide prayer mission to save herself and her people. Her prayers gave the king a sleepless night and forced him to request for Esther's presence. Esther's prayers opened the king's mouth to talk to the favor of Esther.

Esther's prayers brought the downfall of her arc enemy and the enemy of God's people called Haman. Her prayers revoked the decree and brought victory to God's children. Her prayers wiped away all tears from God's people, gave them rest, feasts and promoted Mordecai.

It is an insult to God for his own children to remain at the mercies of devil and his agents. The earth, the fullness thereof and people therein belong to God by creation. Many Christians do not know their rights and as a result, they underestimate themselves, undervalue themselves and allow the devil who is the usurper to subtly deceive them to believe his lies concerning who owns all things. Esther, like many believers, originally believed that she could not do anything.

> 'Again Esther spake unto Hatach, and gave him commandment unto Mordecai; All the king's servants, and the people of the king's provinces, do know, that whosoever, whether man or woman, shall come unto the king into the inner court, who is not called, there is one law of his to put him to death, except such to whom the king shall hold out the golden scepter, that he may live: but I have not been called to come in unto the king these thirty days' (Esther 4:10-11).

It is not God's will for any believer to live a defeated life. It is an insult to accept poverty, sickness or any kind of problem. God himself called us his sons, members of the body of Christ, new creature, beloved of God, brothers to Jesus, temple of God, kings, heirs of God, ambassadors for Christ, peculiar treasure, eagles, and shepherd of the great shepherd (See John 1:12; Matthew 16:18; 2 Corinthians 6:17; John 15:19; Matthew 12:49-50; Ephesians 2:22; Ecclesiastes 8:4; Romans 8:17, 32; 2 Corinthians 5:20; Exodus 19:5; Isaiah 40:31; John 10:11-13).

The agents of devil talk to their master, the devil. When you refuse to pray, you refuse to talk to your God, and God will not do anything until you begin to talk to Him. That is what we call evil silence. I encourage you to pray the prayers here and break yourself loose from evil silence.

> 'Verily I say unto you, Whatsoever ye shall bind on earth shall be bound in heaven: and whatsoever ye shall loose on earth shall be loosed in heaven. Again, I say unto you, that if two of you shall agree on earth as touching anything that they shall ask, it shall be done for them of my Father which is in heaven' (Matthew 18:18-19).

You are not the one who called yourself a new creature, God did. As you repent, confess your sins and forsake them, and stand before Him in prayers as if you have never committed any sin. You must begin to reign as a king upon the earth. King Jesus has the final authority, not the devil, our poverty or any problem in your life.

Any circumstance, attitude, curse or utterance contrary to who God said you are can be changed through these prayers. God is not a failure; therefore, his children must not accept failure. You can use the prayers here to whip the devil, no matter how far or how long he has harassed you in life. When you pray, God will not allow the enemy or demons to defile you, His temple.

No strange fire can last in the life of true children of God, who know and believe what God says about them. We belong to God by creation and by redemption and he watches over us to preserve us. If you refuse to acknowledge your sins, confess, repent and forsake them, you rob God of what rightly belong to Him. So, repent before you go into these prayers of decrees.

CHAPTER TWO

WHY DO WE NEED TO FAST, PRAY AND DECREE?

- Because many people are under satanic attacks and many are now confused, year after year.

- Because of the increase of witchcraft activities and occultism.

- Because many problems are beyond medical science and mysterious deaths are on the increase.

- Because many people are at cross road, hopeless and peace is scarce all over the world.

- Because of political instability and need of national healing.

- Because of unsolved family problems in many homes, the increase of divorce cases, separations and single parents in the society.

- Because of family troubles, increase in unemployment, youth violence and social unrests.

- Because of occultism in the church and demonic attacks on believers.

- Because the church and the society are in need of people of character and integrity, as many destructive bad habits have captured many people in our generation.

- Many need protections from evil forces and they are not getting it.

- Because many great people on earth especially believers are entangled in economic meltdown, lockdown and destructive virus.

- Because of the debilitating and deplorable health situations of many, even with the abundance of food and medical technology in our generation.

- Because of the growing number of youths who are engaged in terrorism, possibly because of unemployment.

- Because of the increase of wars, quest for power, fame, position and love of money among the restless and vibrant youths.

- Because evil men are increasing and wicked people getting richer, and the number of poor people getting higher.

- Because of worldliness, pleasure, and millions of sexual demons and the manifestation of unclean spirits.

The reason for rampant satanic evil invasions today in the world is high level of ignorance in our Christian communities. Christian life has been watered down and standards greatly compromised. Only few people among the professing Christians actually know the true meaning of Christianity and God's demand in many areas of life.

Materialism has replaced the true faith and many are now pursuing shadows. Prayers of deliverance, fasting and prayers for revival are needed in our generation from the leadership to the last person in the church and our communities. Sin, flesh and demonstrations of carnality are on the increase.

We need to go back to the Scriptures and find out from God what is wrong. The burden in my heart as I write this book is to provide insights into various topics of great concern before prayers are offered. Many religious prayer groups and deliverance ministers are being converted to join occult groups because of famine of God's Word.

They pray without true knowledge of God and His Word, do deliverance without righteousness, command power without purity, gifts without grace, discernment without being disciplined and faith without fruits.

Many prayer groups, deliverance ministries are turning to evil gathering of people who perform miracles without mercy, healing without holiness. Many leaders lack God's grace, purity, discipline, mercy, love and other fruit of the spirit, and yet they lead others. We need to know and experience the basis of truth before prayers are offered to God.

CHAPTER THREE

PRAYERS OF DECREES TO TAKEOVER YOUR YEAR

Every year has blessings attached to it, with everyone's name in each of the blessings. Unfortunately, many enter into the year and end it without enjoying any of these blessings meant for them for the year. Today, many people live and die without enjoying a single blessing that God has destined for them on earth. Lazarus was one of such people.

> 'There was a certain rich man, which was clothed in purple and fine linen, and fared sumptuously every day: And there was a certain beggar named Lazarus, which was laid at his gate, full of sores, And desiring to be fed with the crumbs which fell from the rich man's table: moreover the dogs came and licked his sores' (Luke 16:19-21).

In my early life, I used to live like that, depending solely on people's handouts until a relative I was living with at 17, Brown Street, Lagos State, Nigeria asked me a question that would change my life forever. In those years, this particular relative of mine used to keep his old clothes and shoes in a box. When I gave my life to Christ, I could not even afford fairly used clothes or slippers. So, one morning, I requested for some of those old clothes he was keeping in a box. Instead, he asked me, 'When will you start to provide for yourself?' At that time, I never knew that the question he asked me was also in the Bible. Later when I discovered the scripture that addressed that question, I started praying like I have never prayed before and that is exactly what I expect you to do this year.

'For it was little which thou hadst before I came, and it is now increased unto a multitude; and the Lord hath blessed thee since my coming: and now when shall I provide for mine own house also?' (Genesis 30:30).

Today, that question is answered. By the grace of God, not only can I provide for myself, but for others as well. Like I said earlier, I read a book titled, "Day By Day" - English Course' text book when I was in primary school; central school "Agbogugu" many years back. A particular phrase that says, *'Obi is a boy and Ada is a girl'*. If you do not go into prayer of decrees, you may remain a *'boy or girl'* spiritually and physically, year in and year out. Maybe there is a situation that is asking you the same question – *'When will you provide for yourself or family? When will you get married? When will you become a parent, car owner, land lord or be healed from that sickness?'*

God has answers to every question. This book will help you pray targeted prayers of decrees that will give you results. Do not allow this year to pass you by. With this book, you can engage the year as many times as possible, from January to December. You will make it this year, in Jesus mighty name I pray, Amen!

But before you rush into prayers of decrees, you have to repent of all your sins, confess them and determine to forsake them. Without your readiness to forsake all your sins don't bother to go into prayers of decrees because it will not benefit you. And let me tell you, you cannot deceive God or mock Him. He knows the sin you are confessing and ready to forsake. Therefore, if you are ready to repent, confess and forsake your sins, do so now before engaging in this program but if not; postpone it until you are deadly ready to say bye bye to sin. God bless your year as you join us to say enough is enough to every problem attached to this year.

DECREE SECTION

How To Start Your Program

This book is a precious guide and help in your prayers of decree and fasting.

Choose a suitable method of fasting that suits you, as directed by the Holy Spirit.

It is best to handle prayers of decree at late nights or very early mornings, as the Holy Spirit directs you.

You can start your fast at 6:00 am and break off at 12 noon, 2:00 pm, 3:00 pm, 4:00 pm or 6:00 pm; as you consider most suitable.

You can repeat your decrees as many times as you could, both day and night. Again, decrees are effective at nights, between 12 and 2:00 am but can also be done at any time of the day.

May God Almighty hear your prayers and change your situation for the best this year – Amen.

DECREE 1

Every sin that entered into my life this year, be frustrated, come out now. Every problem that joined me this year, I reject you by force, in the name of Jesus. Father Lord, arise and deliver me from destruction. Every satanic embargo placed upon my life, be lifted, in the name of Jesus. Let every satanic activity in my life be terminated. Let the agenda of devil over my life be terminated, in the name of Jesus.

I speak destruction over evil voices against me, in the name of Jesus. Every evil force that woke up with me this year, perish. I command every evil reign in my life to be terminated, in the name of Jesus. Blood of Jesus, flow into my foundation and deliver me. Wherever my star was arrested, I release it by force, in the name of Jesus.

Every curse placed upon my life, expire forever, in the name of Jesus. Every covenant hindering my progress, break by fire. Holy Ghost fire, burn to ashes every pollution in my life, in the name of Jesus. Every evil assignment over my life this year, be wasted. Every evil hand raised against me this year, dry up. Every evil program running against my life this year, fail woefully, in the name of Jesus.

Every evil yoke designed against me this year, break, in the name of Jesus. Lord Jesus, arise and promote me this year. Let that sin multiplying my problems smite my stubborn enemy unto death and die as well, in the name of Jesus. Every evil activity going on everywhere against my life, be terminated. I command the sun and the moon to fight for me, in the name of Jesus.

Every evil movement against my life, be demobilized, in the name of Jesus. Every power assigned to arrest my star this year, be arrested. Every witchcraft power manifesting under the waters against me, fail woefully, in the name of Jesus. Every witchcraft plan against me this year, be aborted. Every messenger of trouble that is assigned to me this year, perish, in the name of Jesus. Let every program of the wicked against my life this year be frustrated. I enter into the air to recover all my lost blessings, in the name of Jesus.

Let my enemies begin to make mistakes that will favor me, in the name of Jesus. Every attack of the devil planned against me this year, fail woefully. Every agent of destiny killer sent to me, perish on your way, in the name of Jesus. Every evil bullet directed towards my destiny, backfire. Every arrow of death and hell fired against me, backfire, in the name of Jesus. Father Lord, arise and take me to my place of rest this year. Every power or personality mandated to hurt me this year, perish, in the name of Jesus. I break and loose myself from all unfriendly friends, in the name of Jesus.

DECREE 2

Every weapon of destruction prepared for me and my family this year, destroy your owners, in the name of Jesus. Wherever every member of my family will be called for evil this year, blood of Jesus answer for us. I command the wind of judgment to visit the camp of my enemies, in the name of Jesus. Thunder of God's judgment, move and locate my enemies wherever they are now. Let Holy Ghost rain of blessings fall upon every member of my family, in the name of Jesus. Lord, take me away from every evil trap, in the name of Jesus.

Every demonic gang-up against me this year, scatter, in the name of Jesus. I command every shame, disgrace and reproach in my life to perish. Every spiritual parent or relations troubling my life, perish, in the name of Jesus. Let destroying flood of God carry away all my problems this year. Every evil eye that will ever monitor me this year shall be blinded, in the name of Jesus. Every arrow of confusion coming towards my apartment, be diverted. Lord, arise and deliver me from fear this year, in the name of Jesus.

I receive divine boldness to approach my problems this year, in the name of Jesus. Every household enemy working against my family, be disgraced. Father Lord, help me to overcome every temptation this year, in the name of Jesus. Every power that is ready to manipulate my helpers this year, perish. Every evil load prepared against me by evil forces, i reject you, in the name of Jesus. Every evil kingdom causing my star to wonder about, scatter. Every demonic dream prepared against me this year, backfire, in the name of Jesus.

Every area of my life marked for destruction this year, be delivered, in the name of Jesus. Father Lord, deliver me from financial crisis this year. Every power empowered to attack my health this year, perish, in the name of Jesus. I break and loose myself from grip of water spirits. Every stubborn problem in my life, receive destruction, in the name of Jesus. Father Lord, bless the works of my hands mightily this year, in the name of Jesus.

Every handwriting of witchcraft against every member of my family this year, catch fire and be rubbed off, in the name of Jesus. Let all my uncompromising enemies receive deadly shocks. Every door of affliction opened against me this year, close. Every evil deposit in my body, catch fire and burn to ashes, in the name of Jesus. Every spiritual armed robber visiting me in my dreams, perish. Let my body reject every satanic poison prepared against me. Every part of my destiny under bewitchment, be delivered, in the name of Jesus. Every hidden oppressor against my life, be exposed unto death, in the name of Jesus.

DECREE 3

I break the backbone of all my problems this year, in the name of Jesus. I command all creatures to arise and honor me this year. Every spirit behind my problems, I cast you out, in the name of Jesus. I mobilize the resources of heaven to arise and come to me this year. I command all my money in this year to meet up all my needs. I command all elemental powers to frustrate my problems this year. I raise God's altar everywhere I go from today, in the name of Jesus.

I command my environments to give up all my stolen blessings, in the name of Jesus. Let the presence of God occupy every space in my destiny. I send arrows of death from heaven to all my problems, in the name of Jesus. I command every evil star working against me to perish. I frustrate all my enemies from the heavenlies. Let destructive wind blow from heaven against my enemies, in the name of Jesus. I command heavenly blessings to flow into my life, in the name of Jesus.

Every negative dream against my life this year, be converted to a positive dream, in the name of Jesus. I bring down to dust all evil stars against my life in the heavenlies. Every evil utterance said against me, backfire. Let the might of God take me away from dangers this year, in the name of Jesus. I receive power of righteousness to overcome sin this year. Let my sorrows this year be converted to joy, in the name of Jesus.

Every enemy of Christ in my life, fall down and perish, in the name of Jesus. Every evil judgment against my life this year, be reversed. Every arrow of incurable sickness and disease in my life, go back to your sender, in the name of Jesus. I command all physical and spiritual idols in my family to be roasted by fire. Every power destroying good things in my life, destroy yourself now, in the name of Jesus.

Every satanic prayer prospering in my life, backfire, in the name of Jesus. Every evil gate that is opened against me, close. Let all satanic angels against me surrender forever, in the name of Jesus. Every agent of shame, disgrace and reproach in my life, perish. Lord, arise and kill all destroyers of good things in my life, in the name of Jesus.

DECREE 4

Every evil leg that walked into my destiny this year, walk out by force, in the name of Jesus. Every demonic plan to waste my efforts this year, be frustrated. Every counterfeit money in my investments, be destroyed, in the name of Jesus. I refuse to be removed from divine program this year. Every evil river channeled into my life, dry up. I command every enemy of my prosperity this year to be disgraced by fire, in the name of Jesus. Every backbone of my stubborn problems, break. Every ungodly program designed to waste my destiny, I reject you, in the name of Jesus.

I cut off every evil hand pushing me away from my blessings, in the name of Jesus. Let evil forces expanding my problems perish. Every satanic minister that will be hired to minister against me this year, become confused. Let all helpers of my enemies have problems that will destroy them, in the name of Jesus. I break and loose my destiny from yokes of failures. Father Lord, empower me to prosper in every area of my life this year, in the name of Jesus.

Lord Jesus, give me an open door that will usher me into financial prosperity, in the name of Jesus. I break and loose everyone in my family from powers of death. Let the fire of God burn to ashes every garment of shame upon my life, in the name of Jesus. I command deeply entrenched problems in my life to perish. Every stronghold of enemies in my life, collapse by thunder, in the name of Jesus. Every witchcraft attack against my life, be terminated. Owners of evil loads in my life, come and carry your loads, in the name of Jesus.

Let all consequences of evil covenant and curses in my life expire, in the name of Jesus. Every evil targeted against me and my family this year, backfire, in the name of Jesus.

DECREE 5

I command divine concentrated acid to pour on all my problems this year, in the name of Jesus. Let raging fire of God burn to ashes every evil force against my life. Lord, arise and frustrate all my frustrations this year, in the name of Jesus. You my troubles this year, be troubled unto death. Fire of God, eliminate every evil force that will rise against me this year, in the name of Jesus. Every cloud of sorrow assigned against me this year, scatter. Let my Goliath die and fail woefully in my life this year, in the name of Jesus.

I command destruction to visit the camp of my enemies, in the name of Jesus. Every dream assigned to waste my life this year, fail. Every stubborn curse in my life, expire. Let my life resist every evil verdict against my life, in the name of Jesus. Let all helpers of my enemies withdraw their help this year. Every power blocking my blessings, die and die forever, in the name of Jesus. You my personal stronghold, collapse. Every suicidal spirit attacking my life, die alone. Every power withholding my progress, release it this year and perish, in the name of Jesus.

Every enemy of my handiwork, I cut off your head, in the name of Jesus. Every evil altar in my place of birth attacking my life, scatter. Blood of Jesus, speak peace into my life this year, in the name of Jesus. Every evil limitation on my way to breakthrough, disappear. Let divine whirlwind carry away every roadblock mounted against my life. Every power that has arrested my star, release it and perish, in the name of Jesus.

Every problem that entered into my life last year, come out this year and perish, in the name of Jesus. I close the doors of my life against every problem this year. Every witch or wizard that has vowed to waste my life, be wasted, in the name of Jesus. Every evil deposit in my life, perish. Father Lord, arise and oppress my oppressors. Every evil bloom sweeping away my blessings, catch fire, burn to ashes, in the name of Jesus.

Every rag of poverty in my life, catch fire and burn to ashes, in the name of Jesus. Every evil leg walking toward me, break to pieces. Every evil power causing me to struggle in vain in life, perish, in the name of Jesus. Let my movements and actions this year be directed by God, in the name of Jesus.

DECREE 6

Father Lord, send your purifying fire into my foundation this year, in the name of Jesus. Every weapon of darkness prepared against me, be destroyed. Let my life escape from every evil gang up this year. You creatures that devil is using against me, begin to favor me, in the name of Jesus. Every enemy that is determined to kill me this year must perish. Every enemy of my progress, receive double destruction, in the name of Jesus.

Every good thing my ancestors handed over to devil, I recover you double, in the name of Jesus. Every power using the sun and the moon against me, receive stroke. Let Holy Ghost fire purge me of every evil, in the name of Jesus. I command every defiled part of my life to be cleansed by Jesus. Lord, show me a way out of all my problems this year, in the name of Jesus.

Father Lord, command Your power to deliver me wherever I need deliverance, in the name of Jesus. Every negative action planned against me this year, fail woefully. Let witchcraft of witches and wizards fail in my life. Every evil tree growing secretly in my life, be uprooted, in the name of Jesus. Every evil river flowing into my life, dry up. Every demonic wild animal eating up my destiny, die without mercy, in the name of Jesus.

Let incantation of the wicked fail in my life, in the name of Jesus. Every witch or wizard that has vowed to trouble me, receive confusion. Every evil brain planning evil against my life, receive destruction, in the name of Jesus. Every power from the waters assigned against me, be disgraced. Every trouble coming towards me, return back to your sender. I command the air to suffocate every unrepentant agent of devil against me, in the name of Jesus.

Let the rain of death pursue my stubborn enemies unto death, in the name of Jesus. Heaven, send deadly lightning and thunder against my Goliaths. I release hailstones upon heads of my determined enemies. Let the storms of destruction increase in the camp of my enemies. You my secret enemies, be exposed and be disgraced, in the name of Jesus. Let invisible arrows directed towards my life backfire, in the name of Jesus.

I vanish with the air of God from every evil prison, in the name of Jesus. I cause terrible confusion in brains of all my intelligent enemies. Every evil counsel against my life, be converted to foolishness. Let my problem be apportioned to all my enemies this year, in the name of Jesus.

DECREE 7

Every incantation, ritual and witchcraft powers against me this year, perish, in the name of Jesus. Lord, let my complete being begin to function from this year. Every evil rearrangement targeted at my life this year; I reject you. Let the earth quake for my sake this year against my enemies, in the name of Jesus. I receive power to do great things this year to the glory of God Let the powers of marine kingdoms release my original self completely this year, in the name of Jesus.

Every satanic program against my life this year, fail, in the name of Jesus. Every evil force presently in my life, begin to leave now, I receive power from God to resist devil this year. Father Lord, impact in me the Spirit of excellence this year, in the name of Jesus. Every evil hand that stole from me in the past, return them. Fire of God, burn constantly in my destiny for good. Let the eyes of the Lord be upon me forever from this year, in the name of Jesus.

I reject costly mistakes devil has prepared for my life this year, in the name of Jesus. I walk myself out from every evil group this year. Agent of premature death in my life and family, go back to your sender. Every evil altar tampering with my life, your end has come, perish. I silence every evil voice speaking against my life. Lord, arise and develop every undeveloped areas of my life, in the name of Jesus.

Satan, may the Lord rebuke you for my sake this year, in the name of Jesus. Every remnant of poverty in my life, catch fire and burn to ashes. Lord, arise and restore me to Yourself completely this year. Every power contending with my destiny, fall down and perish, in the name of Jesus. Every destruction going on secretly against my life, stop. Let floods of death carry away all my stubborn enemies, in the name of Jesus. Every satanic wound in my body, spiritual or physical, be healed, in the name of Jesus.

Let every destiny demoting power against my life be arrested to death, in the name of Jesus. I receive anointing to win every battle this year. Every evil personality assigned to visit my apartment this year, perish, in the name of Jesus. Lord, feed me with the food of champions as you fed Elijah. I command the resurrection power of God to visit my life. Blood of Jesus, speak me out of every bondage this year, in the name of Jesus.

Every strange fire in the dark room of my life, rush out by force, in the name of Jesus. Every problem in my life from every evil covenant, perish. Let all evil reporters against my life begin to speak against each other, in the name of Jesus. Every evil mark assigned to identify me to problems, disappear. Every dark agent contending with my destiny, collapse and perish. Every power that has arrested my progress, release it and perish, in the name of Jesus.

Let the evil forces following me about from my place of birth be destroyed, in the name of Jesus. Every agent of backwardness in my life, be disorganized. Every evil power that has hijacked my finances, release them now, in the name of Jesus. Let all destiny killers working hard to destroy me perish. Spirit of death and hell following Everyone in my family, be frustrated. Every vagabond anointing upon my life, loose your hold over my life, in the name of Jesus.

Every tragedy prepared against me this year, be frustrated, in the name of Jesus. Let all dangers ahead of me this year be removed for my sake. Every evil group redrawing the map of my destiny, scatter. Let shame take over agents of devil assigned against me, in the name of Jesus. Every dark agent waiting for me everywhere, fall down and perish. Every satanic structure, physically and spiritually in my life, burn to ashes, in the name of Jesus.

DECREE 8

Every problem that has refused to leave me alone, die immediately, in the name of Jesus. Let my life begin to escape from every evil captivity. Lord, arise and deliver me from every trouble this year, in the name of Jesus. Every power delaying angels of my blessings, fall down and perish. Every witchcraft pot cooking my destiny, break to pieces, in the name of Jesus. Spirit of death and hell living in my body, come out and perish, in the name of Jesus.

Let powers from my parent's houses expanding my problems die this year, in the name of Jesus. Every evil eye observing my life this year, be blinded. Every power assigned to waste my efforts this year, perish, in the name of Jesus. Every strange money causing financial crisis in my finance, catch fire. Every organized darkness militating against my life, scatter in shame. Lord Jesus, command your river of life to flow into my life, in the name of Jesus. I walk back into my destiny, in the name of Jesus.

Father Lord, show me the light. Every enemy of my destiny in my promise land, perish, in the name of Jesus. Every power that is visiting my life from the grave, perish, in the name of Jesus. Every power manipulating my destiny, be manipulated to death. I reject every counterfeit blessing assigned to waste my life. Every evil umbrella covering my glory, catch fire. Every internal thief hiding in my life, be exposed to death, in the name of Jesus. Let every wicked personality that has vowed to disgrace me be disgraced, in the name of Jesus.

Let every enemy of my breakthrough receive death, in the name of Jesus. Every power that has hijacked this year from me, release it now. Every evil personality that must die for my life to move forward, die immediately. Every evil burial against my life, be exhumed by force, in the name of Jesus. Every evil womb that has swallowed my blessings, vomit them now. I break and loose myself from all manners of captivity, in the name of Jesus.

I release my potentials from the hands of my enemies. Holy Ghost fire, burn all my problems this year to ashes, in the name of Jesus. Lord, let Your divine agenda be fulfilled in my life. Every stronghold of failure in my life, collapse by thunder, in the name of Jesus. Let all my deeply entrenched problems die this year. Every enemy of my days and nights this year, die immediately, in the name of Jesus.

DECREE 9

I command every satanic investment in my life to perish, in the name of Jesus. Every evil program against my life, perish. Let evil pronouncement against my blessings be wasted, in the name of Jesus. Every evil arrest against my position, be released. Every good thing I have lost to devil, I recover you completely. Every spiritual warfare going on against my life, end to my favor, in the name of Jesus.

I speak death against all my problems, in the name of Jesus. I destroy every demonic dominion over my life. I command evil powers sitting upon my blessings to perish. I speak death unto every evil voice raised against me, in the name of Jesus. I pull down every problem that has exalted itself over me. I speak from the heavens against every evil authority in my territory, in the name of Jesus.

Every evil power reigning over my life, be dethroned, in the name of Jesus. Blood of Jesus, pour upon the heads of my enemies. I cut off the head of strongman of my father's house, in the name of Jesus. I speak death to every problem programmed into the sun against me. You the sun, reverse every curse programmed into you against me, in the name of Jesus.

I release destruction from the sun against my stubborn enemies, in the name of Jesus. Let the sun hunt to death every destroyer of my life. You the sun, refuse to honor Every evil word against my life this year. Wherever my enemies are coming from, let the sun smite them, in the name of Jesus. You the sun, revolt against every incantation made against my life. I command the moon to pursue my enemies to destruction, in the name of Jesus.

Every evil thing programmed into the moon against my life, perish, in the name of Jesus. Lord, arise and use the moon to defend my life. Blood of Jesus, arise and silence my problems. Let fire arise from the sun to defend me, in the name of Jesus. Every evil personality working to arrest my life, I arrest your star. Let fire of God burn to ashes the stars behind my problems, in the name of Jesus.

Every enemy of my life, be frustrated to death, in the name of Jesus. Let every wicked star against my life this year by locked up by God. I arrest to death the stars of my occultic enemies. Let waters of death fill the mouths of the wicked, in the name of Jesus. Every enemy of my destiny, be troubled by the waters in your belly, in the name of Jesus.

I command the waters all over the world to fight my enemies, in the name of Jesus. Let the waters on earth and the heavenlies trouble my troubles. I command fire to move around now and burn my problems to ashes. Wherever my enemies are hiding, let Holy Ghost fire locate and burn them. Fire of God, move forward and deliver me, in the name of Jesus.

I command penetrating power of God to use fire against all my failures, in the name of Jesus. I command fire to purge my body of every problem. Let fire of God shine into dark areas of my life, in the name of Jesus. Blood of Jesus and fire of God, deliver me this year, in the name of Jesus. Let shining and enlightening power of God expose my problems to death, in the name of Jesus.

Let the air move towards my enemies' camps and waste them. Every evil air directed against my life, backfire, in the name of Jesus. I enter into the air to waste my destiny wasters. Let the air of destruction enter into the camp of my enemies, in the name of Jesus. Every satanic road block against my life, be removed by air. Every evil power monitoring my life, I destroy you by air. I destroy my problems everywhere they exist and command them to vanish, in the name of Jesus.

Every evil movement against my life, be arrested by air in the name of Jesus. Let the air carry message of death to all wicked personalities against me. I release messengers of death by air into every witchcraft gathering. I command the air to scatter all my unrepentant enemies, in the name of Jesus. Let destructive tempest enter into the waters and fight for me, I walk into the cloud to put an end to every evil work against me, in the name of Jesus.

Let thunder from the third heavens blow off my enemies, in the name of Jesus. I release angry lightening to kill every problem in my life. Let hail stones from God fall upon the heads of my stubborn enemies, in the name of Jesus. Angels of God, release hailstones into the camp of my enemies. Let destructive rain fall from heaven upon wicked persons against my life, in the name of Jesus.

I command rain of death to enter the camp of the wicked, in the name of Jesus. Let rain of destruction visit the sun, moon and waters for my sake. Blood of Jesus, speak death to idols of my father's house, in the name of Jesus. Let the snow of death overshadow my stubborn enemies. Let my sickness die by the dew of heaven, in the name of Jesus.

Whoever makes use of water to fight against me shall die by water, in the name of Jesus. Let waters of God on earth rise against all my enemies. I convert waters that my enemies use to rise against them. Let waters flow in abundance and destroy the camps of my enemies. Let my enemies be oppressed by waters wherever water exists. Let the depth of the waters swallow up my enemies and problems, in the name of Jesus.

I command destructive powers in the waters to destroy my enemies. Let my enemies perish before waters, in the name of Jesus. You the earth, open up and swallow my problems. You the earth, refuse to honor every evil sacrifice done against me, in the name of Jesus. Let every evil my enemies raised against my life be buried in the dust. Every power behind my problems, be buried in the earth, in the name of Jesus.

I command the morning to swallow my problems, in the name of Jesus. I command the night to kill all my problems. I command the atmosphere to kill every evil raised against me, in the name of Jesus. Let all the elements join forces to destroy my enemies. I raise Holy Ghost altar against the wicked. I raise divine altars among the entire creations to destroy my destroyers. I command every creature to rise up and fight for me, in the name of Jesus.

Let bedroom, sitting room, car, office and all places on earth where evil is planned against me fight for me, in the name of Jesus. I use weapons of my enemies against them. Let everything my enemies have turn against them for my sake. I command every environment in all creation to favor me. Let the creatures refuse to walk against me, in the name of Jesus. I command angels of God to fight from heavens for my sake. I bring judgment against curses in my life, in the name of Jesus.

Let the entire creation convert every curse against me into blessings, in the name of Jesus. Every star representing my problems, catch fire and burn to ashes. I bring down every evil star against me in the heavenlies, in the name of Jesus. Every power behind my problems, be arrested, Let the entire creation destroy every physical and spiritual organization against my life. Let whirlwind from heaven blow off heads of the wicked, in the name of Jesus.

I command my personal evil stronghold to be consumed by fire, in the name of Jesus. Let great earthquake locate the camp of my enemies now. I release seaquake to waste all my destiny wasters in the waters, in the name of Jesus. I command the air to quake for my sake and destroy works of evil principalities against my life. Horrible tempest, fall upon the camp of my enemies, in the name of Jesus. Let the furnace of affliction oppress my oppressors to death. I send brimstone and fire from heavens against my unrepentant enemies, in the name of Jesus.

I command madness to enter into brains of my unrepentant enemies, in the name of Jesus. Fire of blindness, possess the eyes of my wicked enemies. Let the bones of my enemies lose their strength, in the name of Jesus. I feed all my oppressors with bread and water of affliction. I command the cloud of sorrow to cover all my enemies, in the name of Jesus. Let the unbearable heat from hell fire, burn my enemies. Let destroying flood from above sweep away my enemies, in the name of Jesus.

Let shock, stroke and destruction visit the wicked for my sake, in the name of Jesus. Let the wind of God take disappointments to my enemies. Let arrows of failure be relayed to my enemies, in the name of Jesus. I command evil worms to eat up all my stubborn enemies. Let all my problems face bitter destruction this year, in the name of Jesus. I send arrows of bitter destruction to all my enemies this year, in the name of Jesus.

Let all my stubborn enemies gather themselves to destruction. Whatever devil has done against my life, receive death, in the name of Jesus.

Let all that agents of devil did against me die forever, in the name of Jesus. Every power that will work to renew my bondage this year shall fail and perish. I raise uncompromising wrath of God against my enemies from today, in the name of Jesus. Let the earth, sun, moon and stars, refuse to answer devil and his agents for my sake. I instruct all the elements to fight back all my enemies from today, in the name of Jesus.

Every evil word that will be uttered against me from today will backfire, in the name of Jesus. Let the cloud, tempest, thunder, lightning, hailstone, rain, snow and the dew frustrate my enemies in the future. Let the entire creation begin to oppress my past, present and future enemies to death, in the name of Jesus. I seal my prayers of authority with the seal of God forever, in the name of Jesus.

DECREE 10

Every evil serpent of darkness in the garden of this year for my sake, perish, in the name of Jesus. Let the resurrection power of God quicken all my dead blessings this year. Lord, arise and move my life forward this year, in the name of Jesus. Father Lord, empower me to breathe in Your full life this year. Every opportunity I have ever lost in the past, I recover you this year, in the name of Jesus. I receive divine creative power this year. I command blood of Jesus into my blood stream this year, in the name of Jesus.

Every information that will make me great this year, manifest, in the name of Jesus. Let my body reject evil plantations this year. You my dead blessings, hear the voice of resurrection and arise, in the name of Jesus. Every hindrance and barrier against me this year, disappear. Every satanic network designed against me this year, shatter to pieces, in the name of Jesus. Let Spirit of favor flow into my life this year. Every evil eye monitoring my breakthrough this year, be blinded. I command everything representing me in the kingdom of darkness to disappear, in the name of Jesus.

Angels of the living God, take me and protect me this year, in the name of Jesus. I command all serpentine powers assigned against me this year to fail. Lord, arise and bless me mightily this year, in the name of Jesus. Every agent of satanic delays in my life, I frustrate you this year. Lord, anoint me with the anointing to overcome this year, in the name of Jesus. I reject partial or temporary deliverance this year. I command poverty, lack and begging spirits to depart from me this year. Every personal invitation I have ever given to devil, I withdraw you, in the name of Jesus.

I command every agent of defeat to be defeated in my life, in the name of Jesus. I take away my name from the list of failure this year. Let every oppressor that is assigned against me die this year. Lord Jesus, remove all footholds and seats of devil out of my life this year, in the name of Jesus. I vomit every satanic poison in my life by the power of God. Every evil hosts that will gather against me this year, scatter, in the name of Jesus. Every evil structure inside my life, catch fire and bun to ashes. Every evil door ever opened against my life, close forever, in the name of Jesus.

Let every evil utterance ever said against my life expire this year, Blood of Jesus, flow into my life and deliver me, in the name of Jesus. Every evil tongue that will arise against me this year, close, in the name of Jesus. Lord, bless the works of my hands mightily this year, in the name of Jesus.

DECREE 11

Every evil that took place in my life last Christmas, die by force, in the name of Jesus. I command every arrow of confusion to vacate my life this year. Every evil plantation in my life, your time is up, be uprooted, in the name of Jesus. I command my finances to come out from every cage. Lord, open my eyes to see what you want to show me, in the name of Jesus. Father Lord, reorganize my life this year by fire. Evil effects of all my pasts, be washed by the blood of Jesus, in the name of Jesus. I withdraw my destiny from control of evil men this year, in the name of Jesus.

Every evil soul-tie assigned to waste my life, break by fire, in the name of Jesus. Every demonic program against my life this year, fail woefully. Every serpent of darkness controlling my finance, perish, in the name of Jesus. Every unfriendly friend assigned to waste my life, be disgraced. Let the heavens open and deliver all my blessings this year, in the name of Jesus. Every masquerading problem in my life, catch fire and burn to ashes, I command the anointing of holiness into my life this year, in the name of Jesus.

Lord, create a new hedge of protection around me this year, in the name of Jesus. Let the angels of the Living God be released into the battlefield for my sake. Let the attackers of my destiny be frustrated this year, in the name of Jesus. Every trap designed to trap me this year, catch your owner. Lord, bless me beyond my imagination this year. Every adversary that will rise against me this year shall perish, in the name of Jesus. Let my God arise and provide a way of escape for me this year. Father Lord, be my hiding place from now to the end, in the name of Jesus.

I command my deliverance to manifest this year by force, in the name of Jesus. Blood of Jesus confront all my problems this year by fire. Let the powers of darkness in my life be rendered powerless. Every spirit of ignorance in my life, expire and perish, in the name of Jesus. Every evil decree I inherited unconsciously; I reject you. Every power assigned to waste my efforts this year, be wasted. Every problem I invited into my life, I cast you out, in the name of Jesus. Every dream of defeat in my life, be converted to victory. Every evil parade coming towards me this year, be demobilized, in the name of Jesus.

Lord, arise and trouble my troubles. Every messenger of poverty in my life, carry your message to your sender, in the name of Jesus. Every strange fire burning in my life, I put you off forever, in the name of Jesus. You my body, soul and Spirit, receive perfect deliverance. Every evil load in my life, catch fire and burn to ashes, in the name of Jesus.

DECREE 12

I pull down every satanic stronghold against my life this year, in the name of Jesus. I break and loose myself from every evil dedication. Every power attacking my life from my place of birth, perish, in the name of Jesus. I break and loose myself from every curse in my foundation. Every inherited covenant in my life, break and loose your hold, in the name of Jesus. Every demonic bondage in my life, break to pieces. Every stubborn structure erected by my ancestors; I pull you down. Every poison in my body, dry up by fire, in the name of Jesus.

Let every unprofitable mark in my life be cleared by the blood of Jesus, in the name of Jesus.

I claim complete liberty from bondage of water spirits, in the name of Jesus. Father Lord, move me away from bondage this year. I command stronghold of every evil powers in my life to break, in the name of Jesus. I drink blood of Jesus for perfect freedom in every area of my life. Every ritual that will be done against my life or has been done, expire. Every problem assigned to dominate my life, loose your hold, in the name of Jesus. Let the backbone of my Goliath break to pieces today. Let every demon assigned to water my life be wasted, in the name of Jesus.

Lord, arise and take me to my place of freedom and deliverance in life, in the name of Jesus. Every strange force attacking my life, be arrested unto death. Let that power that steals my blessing every year perish. Every evil personality that visits me in my dreams, your time is up, perish, in the name of Jesus. Evil handwritings against my prosperity, break. I command evil dragons at my place of birth to vomit my miracles and perish. Every satanic worm in Every part of my life, perish, in the name of Jesus.

Let the camps of my enemies be visited by burning fire of God. I command total restoration and deliverance upon my life. Every witch or wizard that wants to finish my life, be frustrated, in the name of Jesus. I close every door I have opened to devil in my life. You strongman sitting upon my destiny, perish, in the name of Jesus. Every agent of devil visiting me as a friend, collapse and perish. Every evil power diverting my destiny, fall down and perish, in the name of Jesus.

I receive God's power to control my life according to God's Word. Lord, renew Your program for my destiny this year, in the name of Jesus. Every area of my life abandoned by God, receive divine visitation, in the name of Jesus. Father Lord, walk back into every area of my life this year, in the name of Jesus.

DECREE 13

Every power that is not of God in my life, perish, in the name of Jesus. Every evil relationship in my life, spiritual or physical, perish. Let evil spirits against breakthrough in my destiny receive death, in the name of Jesus. I command all unclean spirits to abandon my life this year. Blood of Jesus, enter into my brain and wash my mental storehouse. Every obstacle that comes my way this year must bow. Every good thing that has died in my life, be revived this year, in the name of Jesus.

Every confusing voice speaking into my life, be silenced by force, in the name of Jesus. Every witchcraft material hiding in my life, catch fire. Let every stronghold of darkness in my environment collapse, in the name of Jesus. Every witchcraft animal that will cry against me this year must perish. You my family problems, your time is up, perish, in the name of Jesus. I break and loose myself from every spirit of slavery. Every evil leg assigned to walk into my life, break on your way in, in the name of Jesus.

Every evil attachment in my life, be detached by fire, in the name of Jesus. Every satanic cobweb blocking my life, be roasted by fire. I refuse to take evil decisions this year, in the name of Jesus. I command all supporters of my enemies to withdraw their supports forever. Every careless word I have ever spoken that is now hunting my life, perish, in the name of Jesus. I cast out all territorial demons working against my life. Every evil link bringing problems into my life, I cut you off. Every evil arrow fired at my health, I fire you back, in the name of Jesus.

Every satanic rumor that will rise up against me this year, die before your time, in the name of Jesus. Every evil decision that will be taken against me this year will fail. Lord, send light into the dark rooms of my life, in the name of Jesus. I command my enemies to make mistakes this year that will favor me. Every evil chain holding me down visible or invisible, break, in the name of Jesus.

Every part of my destiny suffering in prison, be released this year. I command all drinkers of blood and eaters of flesh to drink their own blood and eat their own flesh, in the name of Jesus. I walk back into my original destiny this year, in the name of Jesus. Every satanic bank keeping my money, release it by force. Lord, arise and increase my testimonies this year, in the name of Jesus.

DECREE 14

I separate myself and family from tragedies of this year, in the name of Jesus. Let all my departed glory come back in full this year. Every evil personality sitting upon my promotion, perish, in the name of Jesus. Lord, arise and perfect Your work in my life. Every enemy of my peace and joy, die this year, in the name of Jesus. Every evil river flowing into my life, dry up by fire. Every power assigned to prolong my bondage this year, die by force, in the name of Jesus. You my stolen prosperity, I recover you double this year. Every agent of frustration against my life, be frustrated, in the name of Jesus.

Every evil egg about to be incubated in my life, break, in the name of Jesus. Every agent of debt in my life, I reject you forever. Every power that wants to stand on my way this year, be removed. Every enemy of my marriage, receive destruction this year, in the name of Jesus. Every satanic embargo placed upon my life, be lifted. Every demonic garment placed upon my life, catch fire. Let all problems designed against my life this year perish, in the name of Jesus. Lord, arise and empower me to prevail perfectly in this year, in the name of Jesus.

DECREE 15

Lord, restrict my movements this year to Your own glory, in the name of Jesus. Every armor and weapons of the strongman against me, catch fire. Every evil kingdom that will rise up against me this year, collapse. Oh God, release Your angels to fight my battles this year, in the name of Jesus. Every evil entanglement against my life this year, I reject you. Lord, empower me and use me greatly this year. Let demonic bondages in my life break this year, in the name of Jesus.

Every evil label or marks upon my life, be wiped away, in the name of Jesus. Every power that has vowed to wage war against my life, perish. Let the fire of God burn to ashes every disease and germs in my blood, in the name of Jesus. Every satanic traffic warden diverting my destiny, perish. Every area of my life under bewitchment, be released. I receive power to subdue every evil kingdom against my life, in the name of Jesus. Every evil book containing my name, catch fire and burn to ashes. Every satanic handwriting against my life, be wiped away, in the name of Jesus.

Every evil king installed against me this year, perish, in the name of Jesus. I command all hunters of my life this year to kill themselves. Father Lord, arise and expose every satanic secret against my life, in the name of Jesus.

DECREE 16

I command every satanic investment in my life to perish, in the name of Jesus. Every evil program against my life, perish. Let evil pronouncement against my blessings be wasted, in the name of Jesus. Every evil arrest against my position, be released. Every good thing I have lost to devil, I recover you completely. Every spiritual warfare going on against my life, end to my favor, in the name of Jesus. I speak death against all my problems. I destroy every demonic dominion over my life, in the name of Jesus. I command evil powers sitting upon my blessings to perish. I speak death unto every evil voice raised against me, in the name of Jesus.

I pull down every problem that has exalted itself over me, in the name of Jesus. I speak from the heavens against every evil authority in my territory. Every evil power reigning over my life, be dethroned. Blood of Jesus, pour upon the heads of my enemies, in the name of Jesus. I cut off the head of strongman of my father's house. I speak death to every problem programmed into the sun against me, in the name of

Jesus. You the sun, reverse every curse programmed into you against me, in the name of Jesus.

I release destruction from the sun against my stubborn enemies, in the name of Jesus. Let the sun hunt to death every destroyer of my life. You the sun, refuse to honor Every evil word against my life this year, in the name of Jesus. Wherever my enemies are coming from, let sun smite them. You the sun, revolt against every incantation made against my life. I command the moon to pursue my enemies to destruction, in the name of Jesus. Every evil thing programmed into the moon against my life, perish, in the name of Jesus.

Lord, arise and use the moon to defend my life, in the name of Jesus. Blood of Jesus, arise and silence my problems. Let fire arise from the sun to defend me, in the name of Jesus. Every evil personality working to arrest my life, I arrest your star. Let fire of God burn to ashes the stars behind my problems, in the name of Jesus. Every enemy of my life, be frustrated to death. Let every wicked star against my life this year by locked up by God, in the name of Jesus.

I arrest to death the stars of my occultic enemies. Let waters of death fill the mouths of the wicked, in the name of Jesus. Every enemy of my destiny, be troubled by the waters in your belly. I command the waters all over the world to fight my enemies, in the name of Jesus. Let the waters on earth and the heavenlies trouble my troubles. I command fire to move around now and burn my problems to ashes. Wherever my enemies are hiding, let Holy Ghost fire locate and burn them, in the name of Jesus.

Fire of God, move forward and deliver me, in the name of Jesus. I command penetrating power of God to use fire against all my failures. I command fire to purge my body of every problem, in the name of Jesus. Let fire of God shine into dark areas of my life. Blood of Jesus and fire of God, deliver me this year, in the name of Jesus. Let shining and enlightening power of God expose my problems to death. Let the air move towards my enemies' camps and waste them. Every evil air directed against my life, backfire, in the name of Jesus.

I enter into the air to waste my destiny wasters, in the name of Jesus. Let the air of destruction enter into the camp of my enemies. Every satanic road block against my life, be removed by air, in the name of

Jesus. Every evil power monitoring my life, I destroy you by air I destroy my problems everywhere they exist and command them to vanish, in the name of Jesus. Every evil movement against my life, be arrested by air. Let the air carry message of death to all wicked personalities against me, in the name of Jesus.

I release messengers of death by air into every witchcraft gathering, in the name of Jesus. I command the air to scatter all my unrepentant enemies. Let destructive tempest enter into the waters and fight for me, in the name of Jesus. I walk into the cloud to put an end to every evil work against me. Let thunder from the third heavens blow off my enemies. I release angry lightening to kill every problem in my life, in the name of Jesus. Let hail stones from God fall upon the heads of my stubborn enemies, in the name of Jesus.

Angels of God, release hailstones into the camp of my enemies, in the name of Jesus. Let destructive rain fall from heaven upon wicked persons against my life. I command rain of death to enter the camp of the wicked, in the name of Jesus. Let rain of destruction visit the sun, moon and waters for my sake. Blood of Jesus, speak death to idols of my father's house, in the name of Jesus. Let the snow of death overshadow my stubborn enemies. Let my sickness die by the dew of heaven, in the name of Jesus.

Whoever makes use of water to fight against me shall die by water, in the name of Jesus. Let waters of God on earth rise against all my enemies. I convert waters that my enemies use to rise against them, in the name of Jesus. Let waters flow in abundance and destroy the camps of my enemies, in the name of Jesus. Let my enemies be oppressed by waters wherever water exists. Let the depth of the waters swallow up my enemies and problems, in the name of Jesus. I command destructive powers in the waters to destroy my enemies, in the name of Jesus.

Let my enemies perish before waters, in the name of Jesus. You the earth, open up and swallow my problems. You the earth, refuse to honor every evil sacrifice done against me, in the name of Jesus. Let Every evil my enemies raised against my life be buried in the dust. Every power behind my problems, be buried in the earth, in the name of Jesus. I command the morning to swallow my problems. I command the night to kill all my problems. I command the atmosphere to kill every evil raised against me, in the name of Jesus.

Let all the elements join forces to destroy my enemies, in the name of Jesus. I raise Holy Ghost altar against the wicked. I raise divine altars among the entire creations to destroy my destroyers, in the name of Jesus. I command every creature to rise up and fight for me. Let bedroom, sitting room, car, office and all places on earth where evil is planned against me fight for me, in the name of Jesus. I use weapons of my enemies against them. Let everything my enemies have turn against them for my sake, in the name of Jesus.

I command every environment in all creation to favor me, in the name of Jesus. Let the creatures refuse to walk against me. I command angels of God to fight from heavens for my sake. I bring judgment against curses in my life, in the name of Jesus. Let the entire creation convert every curse against me into blessings. Every star representing my problems, catch fire and burn to ashes. I bring down every evil star against me in the heavenlies, in the name of Jesus.

Every power behind my problems, be arrested, in the name of Jesus. Let the entire creation destroy every physical and spiritual organization against my life. Let whirlwind from heaven blow off heads of the wicked, in the name of Jesus. I command my personal evil stronghold to be consumed by fire. Let great earthquake locate the camp of my enemies now. I release seaquake to waste all my destiny wasters in the waters, in the name of Jesus.

I command the air to quake for my sake and destroy works of evil principalities against my life, in the name of Jesus. Horrible tempest, fall upon the camp of my enemies. Let the furnace of affliction oppress my oppressors to death, in the name of Jesus. I send brimstone and fire from heavens against my unrepentant enemies. I command madness to enter into brains of my unrepentant enemies, in the name of Jesus. Fire of blindness, possess the eyes of my wicked enemies, in the name of Jesus.

Let the bones of my enemies lose their strength, in the name of Jesus. I feed all my oppressors with bread and water of affliction. I command the cloud of sorrow to cover all my enemies. Let the unbearable heat from hell fire, burn my enemies, in the name of Jesus. Let destroying flood from above sweep away my enemies. Let shock, stroke and destruction visit the wicked for my sake, in the name of Jesus. Let the wind of God take disappointments to my enemies. Let arrows of failure be relayed to my enemies, in the name of Jesus.

I command evil worms to eat up all my stubborn enemies, in the name of Jesus. Let all my problems face bitter destruction this year. I send arrows of bitter destruction to all my enemies this year, in the name of Jesus. Let all my stubborn enemies gather themselves to destruction. Whatever devil has done against my life, receive death, in the name of Jesus. Let all that agents of devil did against me die forever. Every power that will work to renew my bondage this year shall fail and perish, in the name of Jesus.

I raise uncompromising wrath of God against my enemies from today, in the name of Jesus. Let the earth, sun, moon and stars, refuse to answer devil and his agents for my sake. I instruct all the elements to fight back all my enemies from today. Every evil word that will be uttered against me from today will backfire, in the name of Jesus. Let the cloud, tempest, thunder, lightning, hailstone, rain, snow and the dew frustrate my enemies in the future. Let the entire creation begin to oppress my past, present and future enemies to death. I seal my prayers of authority with the seal of God forever, in the name of Jesus

DECREE 17

I command the ladder enemies are using to climb into my life to be broken, in the name of Jesus. Every good thing I have lost all my life, I recover you double this year, Father Lord, empower me to mount up with wings as Eagles this year, in the name of Jesus. I receive power to overcome every challenge that will come to me this year. Every evil enchantment and divination against me this year, I cancel you. Every spirit of adversity living inside me, come out and perish, in the name of Jesus.

Every arrow of death designed for me this year, backfire, in the name of Jesus. Every evil tree growing in my life, be uprooted. Every evil oath or vow to waste my life this year, be destroyed, in the name of Jesus. Every gate of blessing closed by my ancestors, be opened by force. Lord Jesus, empower me to occupy my place in life this year. Every power that has vowed to confine me to one place forever, perish. Every stumbling block on my way to greatness, be rolled away, in the name of Jesus.

Lord, show me where to cast in my nets this year. Every evil throne controlling my life, be razed down by fire, in the name of Jesus. Lord, connect me to Your divine resources forever. Every agent of devil, sitting upon my destiny, be unseated, in the name of Jesus. Every arrow of premature death fired against my life, backfire. I lose myself and every member of my family from satanic bondages, in the name of Jesus. Lord, empower me to obtain favor everywhere I go this year. Let my eagle of greatness arrested by the enemy be released this year, in the name of Jesus.

Lord, pull me into the tower of Your divine protection, in the name of Jesus. Every evil mouth closed against my progress, speak out my deliverance. Every evil imagination against my life this year, expire. I command my enemies to open their mouths and congratulate me this year, in the name of Jesus. Every garment of shame, disgrace and reproach casted upon me, catch fire. Every family altar tormenting my life, be shattered in pieces. Every inherited covenant against my destiny, break, in the name of Jesus.

Lord, empower me this year to receive all answers to my prayers, in the name of Jesus. Every sickness and disease in my past or my life, come out and perish. Everything that must happen for me to be perfectly delivered, happen, in the name of Jesus. Everything in my life eating up my original self, come out and perish. Every yoke of impossibilities in my life, break to pieces, in the name of Jesus. Lord, arrange and pump your blood into my blood. Every satanic fear in my life, come out and perish, in the name of Jesus.

DECREE 18

Lord, arise and frustrate my frustrations this year, in the name of Jesus. Every negative report that will be used against me this year, be destroyed. Owners of all problems in my life, appear and carry your loads, in the name of Jesus. Lord, send Your angels to guide me into every victory. Lord, arise and replace everything that needs replacement in my life, in the name of Jesus.

Every strange fire in my life, quench, in the name of Jesus. You the backbone of enemies of my destiny, break. Lord, see me through in all my trials this year, in the name of Jesus. Every local demon joining forces with international demons against my life, scatter in shame. Every bad leg that has ever walked into my life, begin to walk out now, in the name of Jesus. Every spirit of bondage and heaviness in my life, break to pieces. Let my breakthrough begin to come without negotiation, in the name of Jesus.

Let all destroyers of my destiny be destroyed, in the name of Jesus. Lord, arise and oppress my oppressors. Every problem that joined my life last year, I cast you out this year, in the name of Jesus. I stand against all longtime problems that refused to let me go. Every evil chain holding my blessings Everywhere, break to pieces, in the name of Jesus. Every conscious or unconscious curse placed upon my life, expire. Lord, arise and deliver me from every evil covenant, in the name of Jesus. Every stranger in my life, begin to fade away by force. Every Judas Iscariot assigned against me this year, be exposed and hanged, in the name of Jesus.

Every problem attached to my name to waste my life, be frustrated, in the name of Jesus. Let all my troubles be troubled unto death. Lord, give me the strength to stand in the midst of my oppositions, in the name of Jesus. Let every hindrance to my breakthrough disappear by force. Fire of God, burn to ashes every problem in my life. Every stubborn situation in my life, be deleted by fire, in the name of Jesus.

God forbid that I should go around the circle again this year, in the name of Jesus. Every witchcraft animal living inside me, perish. Wherever demons will gather today against my life, I scatter them, in the name of Jesus. Lord, deliver me from all consequences of my offensive pasts. Every arrow of failure tied against my life, backfire.

Every evil thing swallowing up blessings of my destiny, catch fire, in the name of Jesus.

Let every problem in my life receive immediate abortion, in the name of Jesus. Lord, fill my life with good things this year. Ancestral spirits, pack your load and go, in the name of Jesus. Blood of Jesus, flow into my foundation now, in the name of Jesus.

DECREE 19

Every evil bird flying against me this year, perish, in the name of Jesus. I frustrate Every household wickedness plotting to overthrow my life this year. Let satanic jubilations over my life be converted to eternal sorrow, in the name of Jesus. Lord, terminate every evil program against my life. Every evil decree made against my life by everyone living or dead, perish, in the name of Jesus. Every evil utterance said against my life in every evil altar, expire, in the name of Jesus.

Every power resisting answers to my prayers, fall down and perish, in the name of Jesus. Lord, deliver me from every ancestral spirit. I break and loose myself from demonic torments, in the name of Jesus. Let the labor of witches and wizard expire in my life. Every evil river flowing into my destiny, I block your way. Let the backbone of my oppressors be broken to pieces, in the name of Jesus. I soak every day and night of this year in the blood of Jesus. Every evil power advancing into my destiny, be demobilized, in the name of Jesus.

Lord, let my sun of breakthrough arise this year, in the name of Jesus. You my greatest blessing, be released by force this year. Lord, arise and develop my brain to the highest level. Every evil devil has planted into my life in the dream, perish, in the name of Jesus. Every power attacking my life from the graveyard, perish. I recover in sevenfold every good thing devil has stolen from my ancestors, in the name of Jesus. Every problem invited into my life; I reject you now. Let unstoppable blessings of God manifest in my life, in the name of Jesus.

Every instrument of captivity in my life, be destroyed, in the name of Jesus. Every evil project in my life, stop. Let the plans of God and His purpose be fulfilled in my life, in the name of Jesus. Every witchcraft curse prospering in my life, perish. I command angels of my blessings from heaven to visit me, in the name of Jesus. Every satanic padlock used against my life, be broken. Every unrepentant enemy of my life, be destroyed, in the name of Jesus.

Every yoke or curse wasting my life, be wasted, in the name of Jesus. Every evil tongue that has risen against me, I cut you off. Lord Jesus, deliver me from the decrees of death, in the name of Jesus. I receive divine strength to prevail over my enemies. Lord, help me to meet with the right people this year, in the name of Jesus. Every agent of disgrace in my life, be disgraced, in the name of Jesus.

DECREE 20

I declare my destiny a no-go area for devil this year, in the name of Jesus. Let traps my enemies have set for me this year catch my all my enemies I break and loose myself from all ancient bondages, in the name of Jesus. Every demonic obstacle in my life, be removed by fire. You the ghost of my past tormenting my life, perish. Every arrow of confusion sent into my life, backfire, in the name of Jesus. Every evil fire moving in Every area of my life, be quenched. Lord, empower every area of my life by Your power, in the name of Jesus.

Every serpent in the garden of my life, die by force, in the name of Jesus. Every evil movement in my body, stop and perish. I receive power to win in every competition this year from above. Let every darkness in every area of my life receive divine light, in the name of Jesus. Every problem in the dark rooms of my life, come out and perish. Let the wonder working power of God begin to work in my life. Lord Jesus, walk me out from every demonic trap, in the name of Jesus.

Every evil eye monitoring my life, be blinded, in the name of Jesus. Every witchcraft confusion prospering in my life, perish. I command every organized dark power working against my life to scatter. Lord Jesus, help me to stand against devil this year, in the name of Jesus. Lord, open my eyes to see my breakthrough this year. Power to recover every good thing I have ever lost, possess me. Father Lord, arise and enlarge my coast by fire, in the name of Jesus.

Every evil transfer planned against me this year, be frustrated, in the name of Jesus. You my evil partner, I reject your relationship in this year. Every evil activity designed to waste my life, fail woefully. Every business designed to destroy my name and reputation, I reject you, in the name of Jesus. I command every demonic appearance in my life to perish. Every Jezebel and Delilah assigned to seduce me this year, be disgraced, in the name of Jesus.

I receive power to stop every evil movement all the days of my life. Every wicked force coming towards my life, I block you now, in the name of Jesus. Let all troublers of my destiny be troubled. Every habitation of demonic spirit in my life, be delivered, in the name of Jesus.

Let lives of my stubborn enemies be terminated, in the name of Jesus. Let Every bitterness in my life receive divine honey, in the name of Jesus.

DECREE 21

You my personal strongman, die by force this year, in the name of Jesus. Every satanic limitation against my life this year, perish. Every satanic weapon prepared against me this year, catch fire, in the name of Jesus. Let fire of God burn to ashes every problem in my life this year. Every evil gate opened against my destiny, close by force. Every shrine ministering failure into my life, catch fire, in the name of Jesus. Let stone of death fall upon my problems this year. You my family's Goliath, perish, in the name of Jesus.

Every yoke of sin in my life, break, in the name of Jesus. Blood of Jesus, sneak me out of every prison. Every stone of hindrance against my life this year, be rolled away, in the name of Jesus. Every confusing force raised against my life, scatter. Let hell fire open its mouth and swallow my problems, in the name of Jesus. You my sinful partners, I reject you all this year. Fire of God, burn to ashes ever problem in my life, in the name of Jesus.

Lord, arise and reduce my problems to nothing, in the name of Jesus. Every Pharaoh of my destiny, perish. Every bad dream designed to waste my life; I reject you in the name of Jesus. Lord, help me to live and not die before my time. Let the true will of God begin to manifest in my life, in the name of Jesus.

DECREE 22

Every evil pursuer assigned to arrest me, receive destruction, in the name of Jesus. Father Lord, reorganize my spiritual life this year. I stand against all forces of darkness raised against me this year, in the name of Jesus. You my star, arise and shine. Every satanic embargo placed upon my life, be lifted in the name of Jesus. Every evil power blocking my spiritual life, clear away. Let the head of my spiritual Goliath be cut off forever, in the name of Jesus.

You my stubborn enemy, receive open disgrace and perish. Every evil mirror monitoring my life, break to pieces, in the name of Jesus. Every demonic arrow fired at my destiny, backfire. Every enemy of peace in my life this year, die in sorrow. Lord, command Your miracles to explode in my life this year, in the name of Jesus. Every evil force surrounding my destiny, scatter. Lord, impact Your wisdom upon my life today, in the name of Jesus.

Every evil visitor in my life, come out and perish, in the name of Jesus. Every weapon of unfriendly friends in my life, backfire. Every uncomfortable area of my life, receive divine comfort. Lord, send Your healing power into every area of my life, in the name of Jesus. Let confusion and destruction harvest lives of my uncompromising enemies, in the name of Jesus. Lord, arise and bring Your power into my life. Every good thing that problems have stolen from me. I recover you double, in the name of Jesus.

Father Lord, transform my life to Your own glory, in the name of Jesus. Every evil reinforcement and regrouping against me, scatter. Every arrow of untimely death fired against my life, backfire. Every evil bullet that has entered into my body, come out now, in the name of Jesus. Every evil personality that has confiscated my blessings, release them now, in the name of Jesus. Every satanic poison hiding inside my life, be exposed unto death. Every evil host that has gathered against my life, be disbanded, in the name of Jesus.

Let my testimonies escape every evil arrest, in the name of Jesus. Every evil chain holding me down, break to pieces. Let the glory of God possess me. Every evil personality that has vowed to kill me, kill yourself, in the name of Jesus. I receive perfect freedom to glorify God all the days of my life. I claim total victory over my enemies, in the name of Jesus. Every curse prospering in my place of birth. I receive power over you, in the name of Jesus.

DECREE 23

Every problem grieving my life year after year, perish, in the name of Jesus. Every bitter water in my life, dry up by fire. Let oppressors of my life be oppressed to death. Let every trouble in my life be troubled to death, in the name of Jesus. Let my case become too hot for devil this year. I command this year to become year of my deliverance. Every yoke of devil limiting my life, break, in the name of Jesus. Let evil mouths opened against my life be closed, in the name of Jesus.

Every fire burning inside me that does not come from God, quench, in the name of Jesus. Every serpentine covenant in my life, break. I command all good things that have abandoned my life to come back this year. God, arise and perfect Your work in my life, in the name of Jesus. Every evil personality controlling my life, perish. Blood of Jesus, speak me out of every prison. Every power preparing to rejoice over my life, perish, in the name of Jesus.

Let my destiny be promoted to next level this year, in the name of Jesus. Lord, order my life to fulfill Your purpose for my destiny. I refuse to walk into the camp of my enemies this year. Angels of the living God, walk me to divine blessings, in the name of Jesus. Let my life escape from prison of poverty. You my life, reject spirits of the tail. Every evil record tormenting my life, burn to ashes, in the name of Jesus. Lord, I withdraw my case file from the offices of devil, in the name of Jesus.

Every power that has captured my progress, release them by force. Lord, introduce me to my helpers this year, in the name of Jesus. I receive power to make progress in every area of my life. Lord, dispatch Your angels into the battlefield for my sake. Every strongman that has vowed to kill me, die for my sake, in the name of Jesus. Every agent of backwardness in my life, receive disgrace. Every dream of demotion in my life, die by fire, in the name of Jesus.

Lord, take me to greatness in this life, in the name of Jesus. Every power that has vowed to change God's plans for my life, perish. Lord, send Your power from above to deliver me wherever I need deliverance. Father Lord, make me a channel of blessing to my generation. Every stone of hindrance in my way, be rolled away by force, in the name of Jesus.

DECREE 24

Let every gap between me and my prosperity close forever, in the name of Jesus. Every stronghold of darkness in my life, I pull you down. Every spiritual armed robber robbing my blessings, perish. Every evil force approaching my residence, scatter in shame. Every evil spirit committee set up against me, be dispersed, in the name of Jesus. Every evil done against me between the hours of 12 midnight and 1am, be overthrown. Every weapon of darkness prospering in my life, be rendered impotent, in the name of Jesus. Spirit of my parents living inside me to destroy me, come out and perish, in the name of Jesus.

You that power wasting my time and resources, your time is up, be wasted. Every evil thing done against my life between the hours of 1am and 2am, be rendered impotent, in the name of Jesus. I cut off my life from every evil inheritance. Let the plans of devil for my destiny fail woefully. I withdraw my name from register of failures, in the name of Jesus. Every evil done against my life between the hours of 2am to 3am, be rendered impotent. Every satanic damage in Every area of my life about to manifest, be repaired, in the name of Jesus.

Lord, take me to divine clinic for perfect healing. Every satanic key locking the doors of my blessings, break, in the name of Jesus. Father Lord, put Your deliverance fire into my life. Every spiritual cataract in my eyes, be roasted by fire, in the name of Jesus. I break and loose myself from marine spirit bondages. Every evil power that has captured my body, soul and Spirit, perish. Lord, increase my wisdom to 100%, Spirit of the living. God, wash me from every pollution, in the name of Jesus.

Every demonic dirt blocking my progress, receive cleansing, in the name of Jesus. Let the glory of God come back fully into my life. Lord, show me the truth that will set me free, in the name of Jesus. Every evil prophecy against my life, be aborted. Lord, take me away from every evil foundation. Power to accept victory and reject defeats, fall upon me now, in the name of Jesus. Every problem in my life on suicide mission, die alone. Let God arise and put my enemies to shame, in the name of Jesus. Every evil pronouncement over my life, I reject you. Father Lord, deliver me from all manner of deceits, in the name of Jesus.

DECREE 25

Every demonic obstacle on my way this year, disappear by force, in the name of Jesus. Every charm and witchcraft attacks prepared against me this year, be nullified by the blood of Jesus. I take authority over every evil force that will rise against me. Let the blood of Jesus enter into my life this year for deliverance, in the name of Jesus. Every bondage of sin upon my life this year, break. Every spiritual alarm raised against me this year, be silenced. Every satanic clock monitoring my life, receive destruction, in the name of Jesus. Let the fire of God enter into my foundation and deliver me. Every evil dream prepare against my life this year, perish, in the name of Jesus.

Every curse militating against my life this year, expire, in the name of Jesus. All parental mistakes hurting my destiny, I reject you all. Every evil structure, spiritual or physical raised against me, collapse, in the name of Jesus. Holy Ghost fire, burn to ashes every evil going on in my life. Every weapon of death prepared against every life, kill your owner, in the name of Jesus. Every evil hand blocking or delaying my blessings, be bended by force. Every area of my life soiled by sin, receive cleansing by the blood of Jesus. Let every enemy of my destiny gather together and perish, in the name of Jesus.

DECREE 26

Every satanic judge installed against my life this year perish, in the name of Jesus. Let the head of my unrepentant Goliath be cut off. Every man, woman or power sitting upon my blessing, be unseated, in the name of Jesus. Lord, take me away from poverty to prosperity this year. Let all wisdom of my enemies be converted to foolishness. Every satanic revival organized against me this year, be terminated, in the name of Jesus. Every evil pit dug against me, close by force. I command all my enemies to enter into the pit and be suffocated by fire, in the name of Jesus.

Father Lord, grant me unlimited favor this year, in the name of Jesus. Every power that has vowed to localize my life, be frustrated. I rise against my destroyers and I destroy them by fire, in the name of Jesus. Power to make heaven and fulfill my destiny on earth, possess me now. I speak frustration to every enemy of my life, in the name of Jesus. Every evil force from my place of birth against my life, perish. Every pollution in my blood, be cleansed by fire, in the name of Jesus.

Lord, arise and command my life to move to the top, in the name of Jesus. Every evil covering my glory, catch fire and burn to ashes. Every evil mouth vomiting strange fire into my mouth, shut forever. Every power activating my dead problems, die without mercy, in the name of Jesus. Let resurrection power of God resurrect every good thing that is dead in my life. Every evil association militating against my life, scatter and perish, in the name of Jesus. Every evil spirit I inherited from my ancestors, come out and perish. Every problem that has caged my life, release me by force, in the name of Jesus.

Let effects of evil places I visited in the past receive cleansing of fire, in the name of Jesus. Every spiritual marriage in my life, known and unknown, perish. Every evil leg walking towards my destiny, break. Every evil counselor in my life, die with your counsel. Every evil conspiracy against my destiny, fail woefully, in the name of Jesus. Let my enemies begin to destroy themselves. Every evil arrangement against my destiny, be disarranged. Every satanic crown on my head, catch fire and burn to ashes, in the name of Jesus. Lord, let Your glory overshadow my life forever, in the name of Jesus. I receive keys to succeed in my life this year, in the name of Jesus.

DECREE 27

Lord, move me away from bondage to liberty this year, in the name of Jesus. Every dream of defeat designed against me this year, be shattered. Let hosts of darkness that will gather against me this year be disgraced. Every strange hand empowered to touch me this year, wither, in the name of Jesus. I refuse to follow wicked ways of my ancestors. Every spirit that will attack me from the grave this year shall fail. Blood of Jesus, flow into every creature and recover all I have lost, in the name of Jesus. I break and loose myself from the manipulation of devil. Every stronghold of witchcraft against my life, collapse, in the name of Jesus.

Every unprofitable covenant prospering in my life, break, in the name of Jesus. Fire of God, penetrate into every space on earth and burn every evil evidence against me. I move with wind of fire into the camp of my enemies to recover my loss. Every evil program designed to terminate my life, end to my favor, in the name of Jesus. I deliver myself from consequences of idolatry. I recover every organ of my body spiritually stolen by devil. Every evil growth in my life, perish, in the name of Jesus.

Every problem that has glued to my life, be cast out, in the name of Jesus. I break and lose myself from pains of sickness and death. Every evil scheme against my life, be frustrated by fire. Every problem attached to Every season this year, I am not your candidate, perish. With my hands, I break every citadel of my enemies, in the name of Jesus. I convert all my past defeats to victory. Every evil bird assigned to harass my destiny this year, die before your time, in the name of Jesus.

Lord, help me to harvest all that I planted by Your grace, in the name of Jesus. Every evil garden in my place of birth, receive deliverance. Father Lord, arise and give me multiple breakthroughs. I expose all enemies of my destiny to death this year. Let every situation begin to favor me this year, in the name of Jesus. Let my foundation begin to vomit evil plantations. I receive power to remain great as God has ordained, in the name of Jesus.

Every weakness in my life, be converted to strength, in the name of Jesus. Lord, arise and remember my portion on earth and give them to me. Every evil personality that has vowed to steal my blessings, perish, in the name of Jesus.

DECREE 28

Every voice of impossibility speaking to my life, be silenced by force, in the name of Jesus. Every problem rooted in my life, be dismantled by thunder. Lord, teach me divine secrets that will prosper me this year. Let my financial life become too hot to be managed by devil, in the name of Jesus. Every evil bird eating up my destiny, die by fire. Every effort by devil to destroy me, fail woefully, in the name of Jesus.

I receive power to be blessed everywhere I go. Every strongman standing against my harvest, collapse and perish, in the name of Jesus.

Let every satanic storehouse release my blessings this year, in the name of Jesus. Every peace in the camp of my enemies, disappear by force. Every weapon my enemies have prepared against my life, become blunt, in the name of Jesus. Let every satanic door opened for my sake this year be closed by force, I close every evil hole in my life. Blood of Jesus, give me victory and seal it with Your power, in the name of Jesus.

Lord, arise and change my destiny to Your best this year, in the name of Jesus. Every evil character in my life ruining my progress, be destroyed. Every demon wasting my efforts in life, I cast you out. Every progress devil has ever made in my life, be converted to failure, in the name of Jesus. Lord, arise in Your power and wipe away my tears. I break and loose my prosperity from all satanic prisons, in the name of Jesus. Every power standing against my greatness this year, be removed by force. Every evil power dining in the table of my life, perish, in the name of Jesus.

Let every grave give up all my blessings buried in them, in the name of Jesus. Every dead work ever done against my life, be destroyed. Every architect of my past failures, fall down and perish, in the name of Jesus. I command every spiritual weakness in my life to be converted to strength. Every power activating evil in my life, die by force. I withdraw divine mercy form the bosom of my enemies, in the name of Jesus.

Every foundational mistake prepared against me this year, I reject you, in the name of Jesus. Every persistent problem in my life, your time is up, perish. I receive divine mandate to destroy my destroyers. Blood of Jesus, speak me out of every satanic dark room, in the name of Jesus. Every evil record stored up against my life, be roasted by fire. Father Lord, cause divine exchange to take place in my life, in the name of Jesus.

Every evil chain drawing me backward, break, in the name of Jesus. Lord Jesus, smoothen my path and take me to the top this year, in the name of Jesus.

DECREE 29

Blood of Jesus, use me to advertise Your divine wealth and power, in the name of Jesus. Every evil limitation in my life, disappear forever. Every satanic stamp or label in my destiny, catch fire, in the name of Jesus. Lord, convert my sorrows to laughter and joy. Every evil movement in my life, be arrested to death. Every hidden enemy stealing from my efforts in life, be exposed and destroyed, I deliver my destiny from Every evil arrest of failure. My blessings will not be handed over to another person, in the name of Jesus.

Every evil hand stealing from my life, wither by fire, in the name of Jesus. I break and loose myself from inherited evil pattern. Every man or woman promoting problems in my life, be disgraced. I command all my shame to be converted to my glory, in the name of Jesus. Every arrow of confusion fire into my life, backfire, Lord, command all my dead miracles to resurrect this year. Lord, use me to move this generation forward, in the name of Jesus.

Father Lord, increase my testimonies this year as never before, in the name of Jesus. Let my dreams this year take me to another level to the glory of God. Every evil force blocking my view, be removed by force. Every roaring lion assigned against me this year, perish, in the name of Jesus. Every evil vow against my life this year, fail woefully. Every evil decree about to manifest in my life, be silenced forever. Let the glory of God in my life increase by fire, in the name of Jesus.

Every foreign soldier approaching my life in anger, be wasted, in the name of Jesus. Lord, convert my nightmares into a blessing. Lord, expose ever lie the enemy has ever told about me. Let the hosts of heaven arise and vindicate me with one voice, in the name of Jesus. I issue a death sentence to my entire determined enemies this year. Every evil pregnancy against my life, be aborted by force. Every spirit assigned to waste my life efforts, be wasted to death, in the name of Jesus.

Every evil prophecy against my life, fail woefully, in the name of Jesus. Every demonic wall blocking my progress, collapse by thunder. I command every evil force with a vow to kill me this year to die in my place. Let my determined enemies die in my place, in the name of Jesus. Every evil force empowered by devil to dominate me, be dominated. I shall arise and shine from this year onward, in the name of Jesus.

DECREE 30

I command every satanic investment in my life to perish, in the name of Jesus. Every evil program against my life, perish. Let evil pronouncement against my blessings be wasted, in the name of Jesus. Every evil arrest against my position, be released. Every good thing I have lost to devil, I recover you completely. Every spiritual warfare going on against my life, end to my favor. I speak death against all my problems, in the name of Jesus. I destroy every demonic dominion over my life, in the name of Jesus. I command evil powers sitting upon my blessings to perish. I speak death unto every evil voice raised against me, in the name of Jesus.

I pull down every problem that has exalted itself over me, in the name of Jesus. I speak from the heavens against every evil authority in my territory. Every evil power reigning over my life, be dethroned. Blood of Jesus, pour upon the heads of my enemies. I cut off the head of strongman of my father's house, in the name of Jesus. I speak death to every problem programmed into the sun against me. You the sun, reverse every curse programmed into you against me, in the name of Jesus.

I release destruction from the sun against my stubborn enemies, in the name of Jesus. Let the sun hunt to death every destroyer of my life. You the sun, refuse to honor Every evil word against my life this year. Wherever my enemies are coming from, let sun smite them, in the name of Jesus. You the sun, revolt against every incantation made against my life. I command the moon to pursue my enemies to destruction. Every evil thing programmed into the moon against my life, perish, in the name of Jesus.

Lord, arise and use the moon to defend my life, in the name of Jesus. Blood of Jesus, arise and silence my problems. Let fire arise from the sun to defend me. Every evil personality working to arrest my life. I arrest your star, in the name of Jesus. Let fire of God burn to ashes the stars behind my problems. Every enemy of my life, be frustrated to death. Let every wicked star against my life this year by locked up by God, in the name of Jesus.

I arrest to death the stars of my occultic enemies, in the name of Jesus. Let waters of death fill the mouths of the wicked. Every enemy of my destiny, be troubled by the waters in your belly. I command the waters all over the world to fight my enemies, in the name of Jesus. Let the waters on earth and the heavenlies trouble my troubles. I command fire to move around now and burn my problems to ashes, in the name of Jesus. Wherever my enemies are hiding. Let Holy Ghost fire locate and burn them, in the name of Jesus.

Fire of God, move forward and deliver me, in the name of Jesus. I command penetrating power of God to use fire against all my failures. I command fire to purge my body of every problem, in the name of Jesus. Let fire of God shine into dark areas of my life, Blood of Jesus and fire of God, deliver me this year, in the name of Jesus. Let shining and enlightening power of God expose my problems to death. Let the air move towards my enemies' camps and waste them. Every evil air directed against my life, backfire, in the name of Jesus.

I enter into the air to waste my destiny wasters, in the name of Jesus. Let the air of destruction enter into the camp of my enemies. Every satanic road block against my life, be removed by air, in the name of Jesus. Every evil power monitoring my life, I destroy you by air, I destroy my problems Everywhere they exist and command them to vanish. Every evil movement against my life, be arrested by air, in the name of Jesus. Let the air carry message of death to all wicked personalities against me. I release messengers of death by air into every witchcraft gathering, in the name of Jesus.

I command the air to scatter all my unrepentant enemies, in the name of Jesus. Let destructive tempest enter into the waters and fight for me. I walk into the cloud to put an end to every evil work against me. Let thunder from the third heavens blow off my enemies, in the name of Jesus. I release angry lightening to kill every problem in my life. Let hail stones from God fall upon the heads of my stubborn enemies. Angels of God, release hailstones into the camp of my enemies, in the name of Jesus.

Let destructive rain fall from heaven upon wicked persons against my life, in the name of Jesus. I command rain of death to enter the camp of the wicked. Let rain of destruction visit the sun, moon and waters for my sake. Blood of Jesus, speak death to idols of my father's house, in the name of Jesus. Let the snow of death overshadow my stubborn enemies. Let my sickness die by the dew of heaven, in the name of Jesus.

Whoever makes use of water to fight against me shall die by water, in the name of Jesus. Let waters of God on earth rise against all my enemies. I convert waters that my enemies use to rise against them. Let waters flow in abundance and destroy the camps of my enemies, in the name of Jesus. Let my enemies be oppressed by waters wherever water exists. Let the depth of the waters swallow up my enemies and problems, in the name of Jesus.

I command destructive powers in the waters to destroy my enemies, in the name of Jesus. Let my enemies perish before waters. You the earth, open up and swallow my problems, in the name of Jesus. You the earth, refuse to honor Every evil sacrifice done against me. Let Every evil my enemies raised against my life be buried in the dust. Every power behind my problems, be buried in the earth, in the name of Jesus. I command the morning to swallow my problems. I command the night to kill all my problems, in the name of Jesus.

I command the atmosphere to kill every evil raised against me, in the name of Jesus. Let all the elements join forces to destroy my enemies, I raise Holy Ghost altar against the wicked, in the name of Jesus. I raise divine altars among the entire creations to destroy my destroyers. I command every creature to rise up and fight for me. Let bedroom, sitting room, car, office and all places on earth where evil is planned against me fight for me, in the name of Jesus. I use weapons of my enemies against them. Let everything my enemies have turn against them for my sake, in the name of Jesus.

I command every environment in all creation to favor me, in the name of Jesus. Let the creatures refuse to walk against me. I command angels of God to fight from heavens for my sake, in the name of Jesus. I bring judgment against curses in my life. Let the entire creation convert every curse against me into blessings. Every star representing my problems, catch fire and burn to ashes. I bring down every evil star against me in the heavenlies, in the name of Jesus. Every power behind my problems, be arrested. Let the entire creation destroy every physical and spiritual organization against my life, in the name of Jesus.

Let whirlwind from heaven blow off heads of the wicked. I command my personal evil stronghold to be consumed by fire. Let great earthquake locate the camp of my enemies now, in the name of Jesus. I release seaquake to waste all my destiny wasters in the waters. I command the air to quake for my sake and destroy works of evil principalities against my life. Horrible tempest, fall upon the camp of my enemies, in the name of Jesus. Let the furnace of affliction oppress my oppressors to death. I send brimstone and fire from heavens against my unrepentant enemies, in the name of Jesus.

I command madness to enter into brains of my unrepentant enemies, in the name of Jesus. Fire of blindness, possess the eyes of my wicked enemies. Let the bones of my enemies lose their strength. I feed all my oppressors with bread and water of affliction. I command the cloud of sorrow to cover all my enemies, in the name of Jesus. Let the unbearable heat from hell fire, burn my enemies. Let destroying flood from above sweep away my enemies. Let shock, stroke and destruction visit the wicked for my sake, in the name of Jesus.

Let the wind of God take disappointments to my enemies, in the name of Jesus. Let arrows of failure be relayed to my enemies. I command evil worms to eat up all my stubborn enemies, in the name of Jesus. Let all my problems face bitter destruction this year. I send arrows of bitter destruction to all my enemies this year, in the name of Jesus. Let all my stubborn enemies gather themselves to destruction. Whatever the devil has done against my life, receive death, in the name of Jesus. Let all that agents of devil did against me die forever. Every power that will work to renew my bondage this year shall fail and perish, in the name of Jesus.

I raise uncompromising wrath of God against my enemies from today, in the name of Jesus. Let the earth, sun, moon and stars, refuse to answer devil and his agents for my sake. I instruct all the elements to fight back all my enemies from today, in the name of Jesus. Every evil word that will be uttered against me from today will backfire. Let the cloud, tempest, thunder, lightning, hailstone, rain, snow and the dew frustrate my enemies in the future, in the name of Jesus.

Let the entire creation begin to oppress my past, present and future enemies to death, in the name of Jesus. I seal my prayers of authority with the seal of God forever, in the name of Jesus.

DECREE 31

Lord, uproot every evil thing that will rise against me this year, in the name of Jesus. Every conscious and unconscious agreement against me this year, be cancelled. Every agent of financial failure that will attack my life this year, be frustrated. Let every spiritual wolf against my life, be paralyzed this year, in the name of Jesus. I command all evil counselors against me this year to fail. Every organized darkness that will rise against me this year, be destabilized. Every power that has vowed to hinder my greatness, be frustrated, in the name of Jesus.

Every sickness and disease empowered to hinder my health, perish, in the name of Jesus. Every stronghold of devil in my life, be pulled down. Every evil power assigned to direct my life affairs, die without mercy, in the name of Jesus. I cut off the heads of marine powers working against me. Every negative transaction planned against me this year, be terminated. Father Lord, seal all my pockets that have holes this year, in the name of Jesus.

I command all my imprisoned potentials to come forth out of the grave, in the name of Jesus. Let the backbone of my unrepentant pursuers begin to break. Every unfriendly friend attached to my life, be exposed and disgraced, in the name of Jesus. Every evil power eating up my spiritual power, be wasted by death. Father Lord, arise and enlarge my coast this year, in the name of Jesus. I command my angels of blessing this year not do depart until am fully blessed. Father Lord, open up every good door shut against me by my ancestors, in the name of Jesus.

Let problems coming from my ancestors be neutralized, in the name of Jesus. Every battle that started in my life while I was in the womb, die by force. Every evil work done against my destiny, loose your hold and expire, in the name of Jesus. Every power opposing my life from the waters, die by force. Every evil arrow prepared against me this year, go back to your sender, in the name of Jesus. Let all my enemies begin to make mistakes that will favor me. I paralyze Every power that is behind all my problems, in the name of Jesus.

Let every organized evil power against me this year be frustrated, in the name of Jesus. Every power assigned to waste my efforts in life, fall down and perish. I take authority over every enemy of my breakthrough this year, in the name of Jesus. Blood of Jesus, flow into all the earth for my sake and recover all my loss. I command all enemies of my life to be troubled unto death this year. I command every disappointment prepared against me this year to fail. Let fire of God burn to ashes every strange fire prepared against me, in the name of Jesus.

Lord, arise and disarm all my stubborn enemies this year, in the name of Jesus. Every evil leg that has ever walked into my life, walk out and perish. Everlasting God, give me everlasting deliverance this year, in the name of Jesus.

DECREE 32

I command all satanic barriers against me this year to be dismantled, in the name of Jesus. Every enemy of my breakthrough this year, be arrested and destroyed. Let warring angels of the Lord arise on my behalf to fight for me, in the name of Jesus. I walk out from all manner of counterfeit blessings into divine blessings. Every evil flow of all manner of problems from my foundation, I cut you off. Every unknown force organizing problems for me this year, scatter, in the name of Jesus.

Every activity of devourers against my life, be terminated, in the name of Jesus. Every good ground I have ever lost to devil, I recover you double. Father Lord, open doors of opportunities for me this year in multiples. Let all evil forces organized to waste my life be wasted, in the name of Jesus. Let fire of God fall upon all powers denying me of my due miracles. Every spirit of depression that has joined me this year, I bind you, in the name of Jesus.

All my caged potentials and gifts, be released by force, in the name of Jesus. I receive God's power that will make me a miracle this year. Every tree of problem in my life, I cut you off by force, in the name of Jesus. Every property of witchcraft in my life, catch fire. I command all parasites feeding on my life to perish, in the name of Jesus. Father Lord, heal me from all the spiritual wounds I have ever received. Blood of Jesus, flow into my life and deliver me by fire. Lord, give me power for a new beginning, in the name of Jesus.

I decree sevenfold restoration in every area of my life, in the name of Jesus. Holy Ghost fire, burn to ashes everything that does not give God glory in my life. Every evil wall built against my destiny, collapse by thunder. I receive power to pursue all my enemies into the Red Sea, in the name of Jesus. Every strange leg that has walked into my life, walk out now. You my life, refuse to be a fertile ground for every evil to thrive, in the name of Jesus.

Every power assigned to wage war against my life, perish, in the name of Jesus. I receive miracles that will shock my enemies this year. Father Lord, give me solution to every problem in my life, in the name of Jesus. Blood of Jesus, speak every incantation against me to death. Every dark thing hiding in my life, disappear, in the name of Jesus. I command every adversary of my miracles to surrender and perish. You that power that no one has stopped in my family, I stop you this year. Every agent of poverty in my life, be frustrated by fire, in the name of Jesus. Lord, take me to my place of blessing in life forever. Every strongman assigned to waste my life, be wasted, in the name of Jesus.

Lord, give me unmerited favor this year, in the name of Jesus. Every evil record against me this year, be wiped out by the blood of Jesus. I frustrate every evil handiwork of devil against me in the name of Jesus.

DECREE 33

Every satanic turbulence arranged for me this year, be disorganized, in the name of Jesus. I command angels of the living God to roll away every stone of hindrance on my way this year. Let all demons dedicated or inherited leave me alone forever, in the name of Jesus. I break and loose myself from Every collective captivity. Every satanic hole in the container of my life, be mended this year, in the name of Jesus. I command that power that changed the life of Jabez to manifest in my life. Let blessings that will embarrass my enemies manifest in my life this year, in the name of Jesus.

Every satanic limitation placed on my way this year, disappear by force, in the name of Jesus. Blood of Jesus, flow into my life and burn to ashes every problem. Every demonic dream prepared to destroy my life; I reject you. Lord, arise and empower me to dwell in safety this year, in the name of Jesus. Every spiritual coffin I have constructed for myself, catch fire. Father Lord, convert me for every day miracle this year. I command my life to accept every good thing this year, in the name of Jesus.

Every satanic garment sown for me this year, burn to ashes, in the name of Jesus. Let the light that will lead me to my breakthrough this year appear. Blood of Jesus, break every demonic circle in my life this year. Every spiritual padlock against my life this year, break to pieces, in the name of Jesus. Let all spiritual label and marks in my life catch fire and burn to ashes. Every demonic curse of bad reputation in my life, break, in the name of Jesus. Every satanic embargo placed upon my life, break now. Every contaminated area of my life, be cleansed by the blood of Jesus, in the name of Jesus.

Every power assigned to mess me up this year, be disgraced, in the name of Jesus. I use divine brush of the Lord to scrub all dirt in my spiritual pipe. Every satanic manipulation prepared against me this year, be frustrated, in the name of Jesus. I anoint my eyes and my ears with the blood of Jesus to see and hear from God. Every problem eating me up while I am alive, perish. Every evil counsel that will be given against me this year shall fail, in the name of Jesus. Every evil decree waiting to manifest in my life this year, expire. Every evil utterance ever said against my life, fail woefully, in the name of Jesus.

Every serpent in my pocket, perish, in the name of Jesus. Every evil mouth opened against my destiny, close and become dumb. I receive anointing to excel above my masters this year, in the name of Jesus. I rebuke every power behind my problems this year. Every blockage to my spiritual sight and eardrum, receive deliverance, in the name of Jesus. Every strongman behind my problems this year, I cut off your head. Let angels of God capture evil powers behind my past failures, in the name of Jesus. Every witch or wizard that has vowed to waste my destiny, by wasted. Every evil hand stealing good things of my life, wither by fire, in the name of Jesus.

Blood of Jesus, speak all my stolen blessings out of evil prisons, in the name of Jesus. Lord, arise and take me to my rightful place in life. I receive grace to live above sin this year, in the name of Jesus.

DECREE 34

Father Lord, give me keys to my true success this year, in the name of Jesus. Every witchcraft manipulation desirous of changing God's plan for my life, be frustrated. Every evil door opened for me this year, close forever, in the name of Jesus. Every satanic limitation to my progress, disappear by force. Lord Jesus, arise in Your power and elevate my destiny this year, in the name of Jesus. Every owner of evil loads in my life must appear to carry their loads. I command all devourers in my life to vanish and perish, in the name of Jesus.

Lord, arise and favor me this year, in the name of Jesus. Every evil speech released against me this year, fade away. Every satanic mobility moving towards me this year, be demobilized. Every evil eye monitoring my life this year, be blinded. I command all environmental powers against my life to die this year, in the name of Jesus. I refuse to fall into foundational sin I used to fall into every year. I receive divine information that will make me great this year, in the name of Jesus.

Every arrow of manipulation prepared against my life this year, backfire, in the name of Jesus. Let my life attract divine presence everywhere I go this year. Every satanic worm eating up my greatness, perish, in the name of Jesus. Let all my spiritual evil attachments catch fire and burn to ashes. Every evil activity in my life this year, fail woefully, in the name of Jesus. Lord, lead me to make right choices this year. Every evil chain in every area of my life, break. Lord, begin to plant all manner of blessings in my life, in the name of Jesus.

DECREE 35

Every architect of failure in my life in the past, fall down and die this year, in the name of Jesus. Every evil factor that leads my past failure, receive death and perish. I withdraw all my activities this year from evil controls, in the name of Jesus. Every power trying to redraw divine map of my destiny, perish. Every arrow of sexual sin fired against my life this year, backfire, in the name of Jesus. Let my year be delivered from hands of evil designers. Every evil program planned against me this year, perish, in the name of Jesus.

Powers that have vowed to eat up my blessings this year, perish, in the name of Jesus. I break and loose my life from wasters of time in this year. Every problem rising from my past mistakes in life, perish, in the name of Jesus. I command the strongman assigned against my finance to perish. Every evil personality sitting upon my glory, be unseated by death, in the name of Jesus. Every evil cry against my life from my foundation, be silenced by fire. I command my destiny to be released from hands of remote controlling forces, in the name of Jesus.

Every evil wind directed towards me this year, be redirected by force, in the name of Jesus. Let the finger of the Lord touch my life this year by fire. Lord, heal every broken and sore friendship or relationships that will make me great. Every demon of anger in my life, be arrested to death this year, in the name of Jesus. Lord Jesus, convert all my failures to successes this year, in the name of Jesus.

DECREE 36

Every evil character planted into my life to rob me of God's blessings, perish, in the name of Jesus. I break every curse empowered to affect my life negatively this year. I disengage every satanic agent assigned to terminate my life, in the name of Jesus. Every enemy of my breakthrough this year, be disgraced. Every satanic messenger assigned against my life this year, die with your message. I reject every satanic storm that will ever rise against my life this year, in the name of Jesus. Every problem in my life forcing me to compromise my faith, perish. Every hedge of thorns on my way this year, catch fire and burn to ashes, in the name of Jesus.

I command the activities of strongman in my life to fail woefully, in the name of Jesus. Let all my enemies begin to have dreams that will frustrate them. I remove my destiny from the grip of household wickedness, in the name of Jesus. Every dead area of my life, receive resurrection power. I remove my name from the book of poor people, in the name of Jesus. Lord Jesus, walk back into every second of my life and deliver me. Every problem that has settled in my life, you are a liar, perish, in the name of Jesus.

I command Spirit of life to enter into dead areas of my life, in the name of Jesus. I recover all my virtues stolen by devil and his agents. Lord, command Your power to lead me to my promise land on earth, in the name of Jesus. Every problem reducing members of my family to a walking corpse, perish. Every power sitting upon my freedom, perish. Blood of Jesus, introduce me to people that will advance my life this year, in the name of Jesus.

Every power assigned to manipulate me out of God's plan, die in shame, in the name of Jesus. Every enemy of my life this year, be exposed and disgraced. Every power wasting my efforts in life, be wasted. Every stubborn enemy living in my family as a friend, be exposed to death, in the name of Jesus. Every evil spirit sitting on my rights, benefits and entitlements, perish. Every stubborn demon vomiting strange fire into my life, die by your fire, in the name of Jesus. I break and loose myself from every evil influence of a strange person. Every evil covenant holding me down in bondage, break, in the name of Jesus.

Every part of my life in spiritual prison, be released by fire, in the name of Jesus.

God, arise and let all my enemies everywhere scatter in shame, in the name of Jesus. I command my Pharaoh to die now, I receive mandate to prosper above life wasters this year, in the name of Jesus. Every member of my family under satanic bondage, be delivered by fire, wherever my name will be mentioned for evil this year, blood of Jesus answer for me. Every evil river that is flowing inside my blood, dry up, in the name of Jesus. Every evil group assigned to mess up my life, scatter and be disgraced. Let the mention of my name everywhere bring multiple deliverances, in the name of Jesus.

I decree that no problem will follow me to bed today, in the name of Jesus. I speak wholeness into my destiny. Let Lord Jesus bless people all over the world through me, in the name of Jesus.

DECREE 37

Every evil ordination prepared against me this year, fail woefully, in the name of Jesus. Every evil roadblock built against my destiny this year, be dismantled. Every evil covering against my glory, catch fire and burn to ashes. I reject Every evil carry-over from my ancestors, in the name of Jesus. Let every satanic limitation coming from my foundation disappear. Every hereditary evil flow in my life, I cut you off forever, in the name of Jesus. Spirit of my parents living inside me to control my life, come out and perish. Blood of Jesus, flow into my root and deliver me, in the name of Jesus.

Every power promoting partial deliverance in my life, be cut down, in the name of Jesus. Every bungalow of devil in my place of birth, collapse now. Let demons assigned to bring evil into my life, be frustrated. Lord, arise and perfect my deliverance this year, in the name of Jesus. Every evil force saying 'No' to God's 'Yes' in my life, scatter and perish. Every property of witchcraft in my life, catch fire and burn to ashes. Every power that has vowed to convert everyone in my family to nuisance, perish, in the name of Jesus.

Lord, open my mouth this year against unreasonable silence, in the name of Jesus. Every arrow of confusion and stupid action fired against my life, backfire. Every problem that entered into my life from the womb, come out and perish, in the name of Jesus. Father Lord, fill me with joy and Your testimonies this year. Angels of the living God, walk me into my blessings by power. I walk out from Every evil group by the power of God, in the name of Jesus. I break every evil relationship that is destined to waste my life. Every evil imagination against my life, you cannot be fulfilled, in the name of Jesus.

Blood of Jesus, cleanse me from evil defilement and demonic pollutions, in the name of Jesus. Every evil vulture or bird flying against my life, die by fire. I soak my life and everything about me this year in the pool of blood of Jesus. Every bad spirit following me about, I bind you to death, in the name of Jesus. Every spirit of Goliath boasting against my life and destiny, perish. Every unrepentant enemy about to succeed in my life, die in shame, in the name of Jesus. Lord, arise and disgrace my disgrace and trouble my troubles. Every stronghold of darkness that has vowed to stop my growth, collapse, in the name of Jesus.

Every evil personality sponsoring failures into my life, be disappointed, in the name of Jesus. Lord, give me power that will close my enemies' mouths in shame. Father Lord, link me with people that matters all over the world. Every evil roof upon my head, I break you down by force, in the name of Jesus. Every power waiting to ridicule my life, be disgraced. Lord, arise and promote me by Yourself, in the name of Jesus. Every satanic judgment ever pronounced against my life, be reversed. Lord, arise and catapult me to the mountain top, Fire of God, burn every document against my life, in the name of Jesus.

DECREE 38

I command every evil altar to release all my blessings this year, in the name of Jesus. Every evil power standing in the gate of this year, fall down and perish. Every evil priest ministering against me this year, receive stroke, in the name of Jesus. Blood of Jesus, speak death to every problem against my life. Every enemy of my prosperity, be wasted by fire, in the name of Jesus. Every evil personality that wants to retaliate against me, drop dead. Lord, arise and deliver me from every evil attack, in the name of Jesus. Every weapon of the devil against me this year, become blunt. I command my heavens to open and supply all my needs this year, in the name of Jesus.

Let my cries this year attract divine attention, in the name of Jesus. Father Lord, sponsor every project in my hand this year. Every serpent of darkness in my foundation, perish. I forbid evil spirits from attacking me this year, in the name of Jesus. Let my potentials receive divine touch this year and work for me, in the name of Jesus. Every evil spirit delegated against my life, I cast you out. Every satanic siege mounted against my life, be paralyzed. Every information about my life in the camp of devil, be withdrawn, in the name of Jesus.

Every evil power obstructing my breakthrough, be dismantled, in the name of Jesus. Every evil traffic warder diverting my blessings, be arrested and destroyed. Every provision that God has made available for my life, I receive you, in the name of Jesus. Every curse placed upon my life by Everyone living or dead, expire now. Every power that has arrested my star, release it by force, in the name of Jesus. Every satanic power fashioned against my life, be defied by blood of Jesus. Every evil deposit in my life from the dream, catch fire and burn to ashes, in the name of Jesus.

Every wicked power militating against my life, I confiscate your power, in the name of Jesus. Every evil power that will come against me from the north, east, south and west shall die on their way. Every aggressive covenant against my life, become impotent, in the name of Jesus. Every evil fashioned against me this year; I command you to perish. Every geographical hindrance to my breakthrough, clear away, in the name of Jesus. I command every internal and external stronghold standing against me to bow. Every evil summon that will concern me this year shall fail, in the name of Jesus.

Every evil committee that will sit for my sake this year shall favor me, in the name of Jesus. Every power assigned to block my way to the top, perish. Every spiritual actor raised against my life, die in shame. Every power that has put a stop in my life, removed it and perish, in the name of Jesus. Every strange fire burning in my life, quench by force. You the eagle of my destiny arrested by devil, be released now, in the name of Jesus. Every power sitting upon my promotion, be unseated by death. Every evil hand scattering what I am gathering together, wither by fire. Blood of Jesus speak deliverance into my destiny now, in the name of Jesus.

DECREE 39

I command the earth to revolt against all my enemies on earth, in the name of Jesus. Every power contending with my life's promotion, be destroyed by fire. Let evil powers that have disorganized my life be arrested to death. You my original self-arrested by devil, be released by force, in the name of Jesus. Every weapon of poverty in my life, I drop you by force. Every marine spirit deposit in my life, catch fire, in the name of Jesus. Every evil leg that has walked into my life, walk out now by force. Every power that has vowed to kill me this year, fail woefully, in the name of Jesus.

Every evil protection against my destiny, be diverted, in the name of Jesus. Every evil movement in the heavenlies against my life, be arrested. Every witchcraft being practiced against my destiny, be terminated, in the name of Jesus. Every witchcraft animal attacking my life, perish. Every evil action against my life, come to an end now to my favor. Father Lord, arise and enlarge my coast by fire. Every evil power on assignment to steal my blessings, perish. Every witchcraft bird flying over my head, perish, in the name of Jesus.

Every evil tree harboring witches against me, be uprooted, in the name of Jesus. Every evil sacrifice offered against my life, expire. Lord, increase my anointing and grace to overcome my enemies. Every enemy of my progress in life, wherever you are, die by fire, in the name of Jesus. Every evil arrow fired into my life by the enemy, be uprooted. Every evil river flowing into my life, dry up, in the name of Jesus. Every satanic appointment to attack my destiny, be terminated.

Every power assigned to cut my life short, die in my place. Every problem on suicide mission in my life, die alone, in the name of Jesus.

Every evil blood crying against my life, be silenced by blood of Jesus, in the name of Jesus. Every household enemy that has vow to useless my life, become useless. Every messenger of death sent against my family, carry your message back, in the name of Jesus. Every rod of the wicked that wants to rest upon my life, be removed. Every power diverting my testimony, fall down and perish, in the name of Jesus. Every darkness in every part of my life, be replaced with divine light. Every problem I have ever invited into my life, begin to get out now, in the name of Jesus.

God, fulfill Your agenda over my life perfectly this year, in the name of Jesus. Every evil judgment against my life, be reversed today. Every incantation against my life this year, fail woefully, in the name of Jesus. Every evil link between me, devil and his agents, close forever. I reject every cup of affliction prepared against me this year. Every evil personality putting me down, be frustrated, in the name of Jesus.

DECREE 40

Every enemy of my divine expansion, be exposed unto death, in the name of Jesus. Every rain of affliction prepared against my life, be diverted. I break and loose myself from the bondage of multiple covenants. I command every destiny pillar assigned against my life to perish, in the name of Jesus. Every evil spy sent into my life this year, be arrested to death. I break and lose myself from the captivity of concrete curses. Every power amputating my breakthrough, be frustrated, in the name of Jesus. Every evil womb that has swallowed my blessings, vomit them now. Every evil bullet inside my body, come out now, in the name of Jesus.

Every demon contending with angels of my blessings, perish, in the name of Jesus. I reject Every counterfeit blessing designed to corrupt my life. Lord, pour Your favor into my life today. Every coffin prepared against everyone in my family, bury your owner. Every power that wants me to mourn this year, you are a liar, be roasted by fire. Blood of Jesus, help me to celebrate this year in peace and development. Every problem that has captured my life, lose your hold and perish, in the name of Jesus.

I command every evil stronghold in my life to fall from its roots, in the name of Jesus. Lord, give me an understanding that only You can give. Let the power to wrestle against evil powers and win possessed me this year, in the name of Jesus. Every evil personality manipulating my brain, be destroyed. Every attack going on against my life from the grave, stop now. Every satanic minister ministering against my life, be wasted, in the name of Jesus. I cast out spirit of tragedies out of my family, I break and lose myself from vagabond spirits, in the name of Jesus. Every evil mark in my body, spiritual or physical, disappear. You my personal stronghold, collapse, in the name of Jesus.

I refuse to eat the bread of affliction. Let destroying flood of God destroy my stubborn enemies. Let fire of God burn to ashes every property of devil in my life, in the name of Jesus. I command my enemies to be blinded forever. Every evil brain thinking against my life, scatter, in the name of Jesus. Let the raging fire of the devil against my life be quenched. Every evil flood approaching my life, be diverted into the camp of my enemies, in the name of Jesus. I command divine whirlwind to carry away my problems now. Let the sea quake and release answers to my problems now. Every horrible tempest designed against my life, be calmed, in the name of Jesus.

Every oppression assigned to waste my life, be terminated, in the name of Jesus. God, arise and deliver me this year wherever I need deliverance, in the name of Jesus.

DECREE 41

Every dark power wasting my efforts in life, be wasted, in the name of Jesus. Father Lord, open doors of prosperity for me everywhere this year. I reject every arrow of marital failure into my life. Every evil mark in my body visible or invisible, be wiped out, in the name of Jesus. Lord, raise divine helpers to help me this year. Every evil womb that has conceived evil against me this year, miscarry, in the name of Jesus. Blood of Jesus, bring me under Your cover from destructions. Every area of my life that is barren, receive fertility by fire, in the name of Jesus.

Every power frustrating my destiny, be frustrated by fire, in the name of Jesus. Every stubborn problem in my life, perish. Every witchcraft attach to my life, be terminated, in the name of Jesus. I break and loose myself from every satanic yoke. Father Lord, make a way for my prosperity this year. Every evil seed planted in my life, die this year, in the name of Jesus. I command every stubborn pursuers of my life to be pursued to death. Every area of my life that is demonized, be delivered. I command my oppressors to be oppressed, in the name of Jesus.

Let every family spirit assigned against my life die this year, in the name of Jesus. Every problem that came into my life through dream, perish. Every attack frustrating me from the waters, be terminated, in the name of Jesus. You my enemies wearing masks to attack me, be beheaded. Every habitual sin in my life, perish. Every power causing me to do things late, I cast you out, in the name of Jesus. Every curse of none achievement in my life, expire. I reject Every arrow of untimely death fired against my life, in the name of Jesus.

Every yoke of poverty in my life, break to pieces, in the name of Jesus. Every enemy against me getting rich, you are wicked, perish. Every arrow of deceit fired against my life, backfire, in the name of Jesus. Every witchcraft animal attacking me in the dream, perish. Every water spirit demon manipulating my destiny, perish. Every evil sleep undertaken to waste my life, sleep to death, in the name of Jesus. Every yoke of backwardness in my life, break. Powers of blockages at the edge of my miracles, break, in the name of Jesus.

Every power that wants me to abandon divine protection, perish, in the name of Jesus. Every arrow of business failure in my life, backfire. Every sexual demon assigned to defeat me, perish. Every arrow of prayerlessness fired against my life, backfire, in the name of Jesus. Every agent of great losses in my life, perish. I command all disasters planned against my life to die this year. Every witchcraft attack going on against my life, perish. Let the backbone of my problems begin to break, in the name of Jesus.

DECREE 42

Every evil load prepared against me this year, be snatched to desolation, in the name of Jesus. Every planned household wickedness against my life, be frustrated. Let every evil deposit in my body perish, in the name of Jesus. I command my arrested star to be released by force. Every witchcraft attack against my efforts in life, I stop you now, in the name of Jesus. Every evil utterance against my destiny, be nullified by the blood of Jesus. I drop every unprofitable load in my life this year, I pull down every stronghold built against me this year, in the name of Jesus.

I command all my unrepentant enemies to drink from the waters of affliction, in the name of Jesus. Every satanic influence over my life, be removed forever. Every part of my life under evil arrest, be released by force. Every occultic power manipulating my dreams, perish. Every evil mouth advertising my life for evil, close forever, in the name of Jesus. Every satanic project going on in my life, stop. Let all hidden oppressors against my life be disgraced this year, in the name of Jesus.

Every evil gate opened against my life, close forever, in the name of Jesus. Let every satanic worm eating up my life perish. Blood of Jesus locate and destroy every problem assigned to waste me at night. I disorganize organized evil movement working against my life. I fire back every arrow of confusion fired against my life. Let my problems face bitter destruction this year, in the name of Jesus. Every evil prophesy against me this year, be aborted by fire. Let God arise and restore all my loss from my birth, in the name of Jesus.

I command all intelligent enemies to make mistakes, in the name of Jesus. I convert the joy of satanic people in my life to become tears. Lord, arise in Your power and terminate my all suffering, in the name of Jesus. Every messenger of death looking for me this year, be blinded. I reject and renounce every spirit against prosperity in my life. Every strongman empowered to kill me this year, kill your senders, in the name of Jesus. Every property of water spirit in my body, catch fire. Blood of Jesus flow into every second of this year and deliver me, in the name of Jesus.

Let soldiers of God locate and destroy every work of devil in my life, in the name of Jesus. I break the head of witchcraft powers in my life. Every damage done against my destiny by marine powers, be repaired, in the name of Jesus. Every satanic key locking up my destiny inside the waters, break. Every Goliath in my place of birth that refused to let me go, perish, in the name of Jesus. Every part of my life in the altar of evil ones, come out by force. I withdraw my entire life from the captivity of evil ones, in the name of Jesus.

Every evil decree against my life, be reversed. Every evil personality that has vowed to kill me at all cost, kill yourself, in the name of Jesus. I fire back every arrow of sickness fired into my life, in the name of Jesus. God, arise and bless me mightily this year, in the name of Jesus.

DECREE 43

Every death contract or assignment against my life, kill your sender and perish, in the name of Jesus. Every space my ancestors have lost to devil, I recover you double. Every failure and defeat waiting to manifest in my life, perish. Blood of Jesus, wipe away every bad reputation in my life, in the name of Jesus. Let the backbone of all evil covenants in my life break. Every serpentine attack against my life, be terminated. I command every dragon assigned against me to perish, in the name of Jesus.

Let every flying serpent empowered to destroy me perish, in the name of Jesus. Every power behind the curses prospering in my life, die in disgrace. Every evil tree representing me everywhere, be uprooted, in the name of Jesus. Every evil judgment passed against my life, be reversed. Every witchcraft animal programmed into my life, come out and perish. I break and loose myself from evil captivity. Every evil prospering in my life, be converted to good, in the name of Jesus. Every negative action about to manifest in my life, perish. Every evil desire, thoughts and imagination in my life, come out and perish, in the name of Jesus.

Every sexual demon that has vowed to disgrace me, be disgraced, in the name of Jesus. Every agent of Satan that has vowed to destroy me, destroy yourself. Every evil influence against my life, perish, in the name of Jesus. Lord, arise and deliver me from strange woman or man. I refuse to dance the devil's dance. I stop every satanic progress in my life and I recover all my loss, in the name of Jesus. I command the rising god of the wicked against my life to perish. Every affliction that wants to rise the second time in my life, die forever, in the name of Jesus.

I break and lose myself from evil controls, in the name of Jesus. Fire of God, burn to ashes every parental curse in my life. Every power that has vowed to altar God's plan for my life, perish, in the name of Jesus. Every demonic sacrifice ever done against my life, expire. I reject Every satanic gift designed to waste my life. I withdraw my life from sexual traps, in Jesus name. Every incision in my life bringing in evil spirits, drink the blood of Jesus and perish, in the name of Jesus. Every evil transferred into my life, come out and perish. Every idol attacking my destiny, be wasted by fire. I withdraw my destiny from every evil altar, in the name of Jesus.

Every power that has captured my glory, release it by force, in the name of Jesus. Every satanic priest that has been contracted to destroy me, destroy your sender. Every evil river flowing into my life, dry up by fire, in the name of Jesus. Every good thing the enemy has stolen from me, I recover you. I walk out by force from evil places - spiritual or physical. Every power that has been assigned to kill and bury me, die now, in the name of Jesus.

DECREE 44

Lord, arise and secure every second of this year for me, in the name of Jesus. Every wicked utterance ever said against my life by everyone living or dead, expire. I trample upon Satan and all his agents this year. I break and loose myself from every weakness this year. Let the blood of Jesus stand against all my problems this year, in the name of Jesus. I receive power to overcome all evil spirits that will attack m this year. Father Lord, open my eye, to see Your provisions in every area of my life. Holy Spirit, guide me to the place of my blessings this year, in the name of Jesus.

Every witchcraft mouth eating up my destiny, close forever, in the name of Jesus. I receive every blessing that will glorify God and give me joy this year. I cast out evil spirits assigned to deny me of my blessings. I tear down and burn to ashes every evil structure inside my life. Every power causing my efforts to be harvested by others, perish, in the name of Jesus. Lord, show me where to sow my seed this year. I receive the grace of God to make great progresses this year. Every witch or wizard that has vowed to frustrate my life, be frustrated, in the name of Jesus.

Every enemy of my sound health, fall down and perish, in the name of Jesus. Every stubborn pursuer assigned to pursue me to the grave, perish. I fire back every arrow of poverty fired against my life. Lord, arise and convert all my past defeats to victory, in the name of Jesus. Every power assigned to arrest answers to my prayers, be arrested. Let the brain of my stubborn Pharaoh scatter. Every occultic grand master trading with my destiny, perish, in the name of Jesus.

Every evil spirit that refuse to let me go free, come out by force, in the name of Jesus. I command the heavens to release my entire breakthrough. I receive power to trust God in every situation, in the name of Jesus. Every darkness inside me, disappear. Lord, empower me to disgrace all my enemies this year, in the name of Jesus. Every trouble that wants to trouble me this year, die immediately. Father Lord, restore me to Your original purpose this year, in the name of Jesus.

Every satanic investment in my life, catch fire and burn to ashes, in the name of Jesus. I command my destiny to leave every evil place spiritual and physical. I withdraw my life in every way I have handed it to devil in the past, in the name of Jesus. Every weapon of devil formed against my life, catch fire and perish. Every satanic calendar for my life, catch fire and burn to ashes, in the name of Jesus. Every satanic poison in every area of my life, dry up. Every evil hand siphoning my blessings, receive death now. Let devices of all my enemies turn around and waste my enemies, in the name of Jesus.

I command deliverance fire of God to deliver me now, in the name of Jesus. Let all my enemies lose support from everywhere, in the name of Jesus.

DECREE 45

Command every legal ground that evil spirits have in my life to be destroyed, in the name of Jesus. Every generational curse in my life resulting from sins of idolatry, lose your hold over my life. Every power using my placenta to manipulate my life, perish. I break and loose myself from every conscious and unconscious evil soul-tie, in the name of Jesus. Every covenant with water spirits in my life, break. Every evil power assembled against my destiny, scatter, in the name of Jesus.

Every witchcraft spirit inside my life, come out and perish, in the name of Jesus. Every demon attached to my family idol attacking my life, I cast you out. Every serpentine spirit following me about, perish. Every evil bird crying against my life, be silenced forever, in the name of Jesus. Every satanic debt collector visiting my life with my problems, perish. Lord, use me to get to a level nobody has reached before. Every evil kingdom that nobody has conquered before, I subdue you now, in the name of Jesus.

Every demonic family embargo in my life, be lifted by force, in the name of Jesus. Let all good things stolen by ancestral evil spirits from my fore-fathers be restored. Every ancestral lifestyle designed to water my destiny, become powerless. Every satanic limitation holding me down in a particular level, disappear. Every evil hand shedding blood against my destiny, be stopped by blood of Jesus, in the name of Jesus. Every ancient chain of bondage in my life, break to pieces. Every evil gang-up of ancestral demons against my life, fail woefully, in the name of Jesus.

DECREE 46

Every satanic agent, pretending to be my friend, be exposed and disgraced, in the name of Jesus. Every evil power assigned to lead me into bondage, be disgraced. Every evil group praying against my progress, scatter. Every evil spirit I have cast out trying to come back to every member of my family, be destroyed forever, in the name of Jesus. From hence forth, I forbid evil spirits from operating in my life. I shield my life and that of every member of my family from satanic attacks. I withdraw my strength from every useless activity, in the name of Jesus.

Every power assigned to frustrate my successes, depart and perish, in the name of Jesus. Every power promoting disfavor in my life, perish. You that rising affliction in my family, I cut off your head, in the name of Jesus. Every assignment of familiar spirits in my family, expire. Every power spreading my name for evil, perish. Let the assembly of witchcraft powers against me scatter, in the name of Jesus. Every satanic agent hiding under cover to attack me, perish. Every evil head raised against me, be beheaded, in the name of Jesus.

I command all spiritual wickedness against my life in the heavenlies to perish, in the name of Jesus. Every good thing carted away from my life through my weaknesses, be recovered double. Lord, arise and deliver me now, in the name of Jesus. I refuse to come under dominion of my household wickedness, I break the flow of Every family problem into my life. Every influence of Every strange woman in my life, perish, in the name of Jesus. I break and loose myself from every satanic cage of my father's house. I reject every satanic blessing designed to waste my destiny, in the name of Jesus.

Every evil label, mark or stamp in my life, be roasted by fire, in the name of Jesus. Blood of Jesus, encircle my life against Every evil flow. I reject every disease sent into my life to disgrace me. Every satanic door opened to destroy my life, close forever, in the name of Jesus. Every evil attack prepared to attack me at nights in this year, fail. Lord, receive me as Your child forever, in the name of Jesus. Every evil leg that has walked into the apartment of my life, walk out now. Every evil spirit that has brought me into evil bondage, loose your hold, in the name of Jesus.

Every seed of fear planted into my life, catch fire and perish, in the name of Jesus. Let the head of evil in my family fail woefully in my life. The problem people dreaded in my generation will fail in my life. Every stubborn failure prepared against me this year, I reject you, in the name of Jesus. Every evil mouth in my foundation vomiting problem, die and die again. I withdraw my name from the register of devil in this generation, in the name of Jesus.

DECREE 47

I command the spirit of death assigned against me and my family this year to kill the sender, in the name of Jesus. Every voice of sin and witchcraft crying against my life, be silenced. Every evil group occupying my promise land, vacate and perish, in the name of Jesus. Let my heaven open and release all manner of blessings into my life. Lord, bring all my enemies under me this year, in the name of Jesus. Every water spirit agent empowered to destroy me, destroy yourself this year. Every power inside me contrary to the power of God, come out and perish. Every weapon fashioned against me and my family this year, fail, in the name of Jesus.

Every power from the waters empowered to intimidate me, perish, in the name of Jesus. Let angels of my blessing bring my blessing to my door steps. Every evil handwriting against my life, be nullified by the blood of Jesus. I hide my life and that of my family deeper in Christ forever, in the name of Jesus. Let the assembly of the wicked everywhere against me scatter. Every territorial destroyer assigned against my life, die in shame, I command all my stubborn enemies to become enemies to themselves. Every evil arrangement against my life, scatter in shame, in the name of Jesus. Every immoral demon working against my life, perish. Blood of Jesus, speak me out of every problem, in the name of Jesus.

Every yoke of impossibility in my life, break to pieces now, in the name of Jesus. I banish every problem in my foundation from manifesting in my life. Every evil rising against me from every evil kingdom, be suppressed, in the name of Jesus. Every evil neighbor that has vowed to waste my life, perish. Every strongman in my place of work getting ready to waste my life, perish. Every evil covenant militating against my life, break to piece, in the name of Jesus. Every evil bullet fired to destroy my life, return to your sender. Every enchantment bringing fears into my life, expire, in the name of Jesus.

I command every demonic conspiracy against my life to fail woefully. Every evil leg walking in Every evil altar against me, break, in the name of Jesus. Let all efforts of devil to destroy my life be useless. Every evil document Everywhere against my life, catch fire and burn to ashes, in the name of Jesus. Let my greatness receive divine increase and power to prevail. Lord, arise in Your power and give me Your uncompromising support, in the name of Jesus.

Let all those who will support me arise and fight for me this year. Doors of my breakthrough and financial success, open wider this year, in the name of Jesus. Every environmental enemy, wherever you are now, receive destruction. Every enemy that refused to accept defeat, die in shame. You the miracle that will never expire, begin to manifest in my life, in the name of Jesus. Lord, arise and perfect Your deliverance in my life, in the name of Jesus.

DECREE 48

Heavenly fire fighters, quench every strange fire in my life, in the name of Jesus. Every unfriendly friend that has vowed to finish me, be exposed to death. Every destroyer of great people assigned to destroy me, destroy yourself. I command every spirit of Goliath challenging me to perish, in the name of Jesus. Let every spirit of Herod in my life be disgraced by fire. I command all my spiritual enemies to fall into the Red Sea. Let my physical enemies begin to kill themselves, in the name of Jesus.

Every evil power rising from my place of birth against me, perish, in the name of Jesus. Every arrow of mistake fired against my life; I fire you back. Every inherited bondage in my life, break by fire, in the name of Jesus. Every evil sleep being undertaken to mess up my life, be converted to death. Every program designed to change my destiny, be converted to death. I recover all blessings ever stolen from me while at sleep, in the name of Jesus.

Every area of my life that is leaking, be sealed up by fire, in the name of Jesus. Every satanic agent monitoring my life, receive confusion. Let God's voice confront and conquer every evil voice in my life. Every satanic reverse gear against my life, scatter, in the name of Jesus. Every strange touch to manipulate my destiny, fail now. Blood of Jesus, silence all the plans of my enemies. Every stranger that has entered into my life, come out and perish. Let every abnormal thing inside my body receive divine deliverance, in the name of Jesus.

Let the blood of Jesus trouble my troubles to death today, in the name of Jesus. I break and loose myself form every bondage. Let every inherited curse and covenant break by fire. Every information devil is seeking for to waste my life, I withhold you, in the name of Jesus. Every dream that has polluted my foundation, loose your hold. Every evil hand stealing from my life, break to pieces. I close every door household enemies have opened in my life, in the name of Jesus.

Every evil consumption tormenting my life, I vomit you by force, in the name of Jesus. I receive power to stand against devil and his agents everywhere. Every problem irritating my life, perish. I break and loose my destiny from the spirit of failure, in the name of Jesus. Every destructive lifestyle in my life, I reject you now. Let the stronghold of devil in my life collapse. Every evil voice summoning me inside the waters, I refuse to answer. Every garment of shame in my life, burn to ashes, in the name of Jesus.

Every poison circulating inside my body, catch fire and perish, in the name of Jesus. Every satanic blockage in my life, perish, Lord, by Your power take me away from every danger, in the name of Jesus.

DECREE 49

I confess with my mouth that nothing shall be impossible for me this year, in the name of Jesus. Every evil visit assigned to harm my life; I stop you. Every evil establishment in my life, be destroyed by fire. Every road of prosperity closed against my life, open by fire, in the name of Jesus. I receive the anointing to prevail over my enemies. Power to excel and be at the top forever, possess me. Every demonic limitation in my life, I kick you away, in the name of Jesus. Every disfavoring spirit working against my life, perish. Every of my blessings already in the grave, resurrect by force, in the name of Jesus.

Every power that wants me to serve my enemies, perish, in the name of Jesus. I recall all my blessings lost to water spirits. Lord, give me the ability to receive all my lost glory. I command my enemy's unity against me to be punctured. Every serpent in my life, I render you powerless, in the name of Jesus. Every spiritual parasite in my life, catch fire and burn to ashes. Every wicked animal eating me up vomit me and perish, in the name of Jesus.

Blood of Jesus, enter into the camp of my stubborn enemies and kill them, in the name of Jesus. Holy Ghost fire, burn to ashes every enemy of my progress. I receive grace to walk above my limits. Every satanic house in my place of birth harboring evil spirits, collapse, in the name of Jesus. I chase away every evil spirit in my place of birth. Lord, arise and promote my destiny above my imagination. Every evil force standing against my progress, scatter, in the name of Jesus.

Every evil pollution in my life, receive cleansing, in the name of Jesus. I convert my life to divine fire. Father Lord, break me, mold me and empower me to make it this year, in the name of Jesus. Every wicked blood in my true blood, be dried up. Father Lord, liberate my life from destruction. Every evil report against my life, die and give way to good report, in the name of Jesus. Every power that has captured my desire for good, release it now. Let my life become too hot for every problem to live in, in the name of Jesus.

Every demonic arrest over my life, be destroyed, in the name of Jesus. Every demon against progress in my life, destroy yourself now. Every key locking up my destiny, I break you open now, in the name of Jesus. Lord, feed me Yourself today and make me greatly great. I receive keys that will unlock every good thing for my sake, Lord, envelope me with your glory, in the name of Jesus.

DECREE 50

Every wound I have ever sustained in life spiritually, be healed, in the name of Jesus. Every evil voice blocking me from hearing God's voice, perish. I rebuke every devourer in my life, in the name of Jesus. Power to capture my enemies alive and kill them, possess me. I receive power to resist devil until he bows and flees, in the name of Jesus. I command every serpent of sexual perversion in my life to perish. Every serpent of sex without satisfaction in my life, perish. Every strange spirit in my sexual organ, come out and perish, in the name of Jesus.

Lord, show me where to go in life so that I can prosper, in the name of Jesus. Father Lord, bless every work of my hand today. You the handiwork of my household enemy, be wasted. Lord, give me wisdom that will overthrow the wisdom of devil in my life. I command my helpers to begin to help me in every area of my life, in the name of Jesus. I command legs of my enemies to be broken forever. Every circle of failure in my life, break, in the name of Jesus.

I refuse every curse walking towards me. You my mouth, open and speak life into my life, in the name of Jesus. I refuse to negotiate with failure this year. Every arrow of compromise in my life, perish. Blood of Jesus, help me to live right with God this year, in the name of Jesus. Holy Ghost fire, burn all my problems to ashes. I shall arise and shine above my equals, I receive all my lost potentials by force, in the name of Jesus.

DECREE 51

I command every satanic investment in my life to perish, in the name of Jesus. Every evil program against my life, perish. Let evil pronouncement against my blessings be wasted. Every evil arrest against my position, be released, in the name of Jesus. Every good thing I have lost to devil, I recover you completely. Every spiritual warfare going on against my life, end to my favor. I speak death against all my problems. I destroy every demonic dominion over my life. I command evil powers sitting upon my blessings to perish, in the name of Jesus.

I speak death unto every evil voice raised against me, in the name of Jesus. I pull down every problem that has exalted itself over me. I speak from the heavens against every evil authority in my territory. Every evil power reigning over my life, be dethroned, in the name of Jesus. Blood of Jesus, pour upon the heads of my enemies. I cut off the head of strongman of my father's house. I speak death to every problem programmed into the sun against me, in the name of Jesus.

You the sun, reverse every curse programmed into you against me, in the name of Jesus. I release destruction from the sun against my stubborn enemies. Let the sun hunt to death every destroyer of my life. You the sun, refuse to honor Every evil word against my life this year, in the name of Jesus. Wherever my enemies are coming from, let sun smite them. You the sun, revolt against every incantation made against my life, in the name of Jesus. I command the moon to pursue my enemies to destruction. Every evil thing programmed into the moon against my life, perish, in the name of Jesus.

Lord, arise and use the moon to defend my life, in the name of Jesus. Blood of Jesus, arise and silence my problems. Let fire arise from the sun to defend me, in the name of Jesus. Every evil personality working to arrest my life, I arrest your star. Let fire of God burn to ashes the stars behind my problems. Every enemy of my life, be frustrated to death, in the name of Jesus. Let every wicked star against my life this year by locked up by God. I arrest to death the stars of my occultic enemies, in the name of Jesus.

Let waters of death fill the mouths of the wicked, in the name of Jesus. Every enemy of my destiny, be troubled by the waters in your belly. I command the waters all over the world to fight my enemies, in the name of Jesus. Let the waters on earth and the heavenlies trouble my troubles. I command fire to move around now and burn my problems to ashes. Wherever my enemies are hiding, let Holy Ghost fire locate and burn them, in the name of Jesus. Fire of God, move forward and deliver me. I command penetrating power of God to use fire against all my failures, in the name of Jesus.

I command fire to purge my body of every problem, in the name of Jesus. Let fire of God shine into dark areas of my life. Blood of Jesus and fire of God, deliver me this year. Let shining and enlightening power of God expose my problems to death, in the name of Jesus. Let the air move towards my enemies' camps and waste them. Every evil air directed against my life, backfire. I enter into the air to waste my destiny wasters, in the name of Jesus. Let the air of destruction enter into the camp of my enemies. Every satanic road block against my life, be removed by air, in the name of Jesus.

Every evil power monitoring my life, I destroy you by air, in the name of Jesus. I destroy my problems everywhere they exist and command them to vanish. Every evil movement against my life, be arrested by air. Let the air carry message of death to all wicked personalities against me. I release messengers of death by air into every witchcraft gathering, in the name of Jesus. I command the air to scatter all my unrepentant enemies. Let destructive tempest enter into the waters and fight for me. I walk into the cloud to put an end to every evil work against me, in the name of Jesus. Let thunder from the third heavens blow off my enemies, in the name of Jesus.

I release angry lightening to kill every problem in my life, in the name of Jesus. Let hail stones from God fall upon the heads of my stubborn enemies, in the name of Jesus. Angels of God, release hailstones into the camp of my enemies. Let destructive rain fall from heaven upon wicked persons against my life. I command rain of death to enter the camp of the wicked, in the name of Jesus. Let rain of destruction visit the sun, moon and waters for my sake. Blood of Jesus, speak death to idols of my father's house, in the name of Jesus.

Let the snow of death overshadow my stubborn enemies, in the name of Jesus. Let my sickness die by the dew of heaven. Whoever makes use of water to fight against me shall die by water, in the name of

Jesus. Let waters of God on earth rise against all my enemies. I convert waters that my enemies use to rise against them. Let waters flow in abundance and destroy the camps of my enemies, in the name of Jesus. Let my enemies be oppressed by waters wherever water exists. Let the depth of the waters swallow up my enemies and problems, in the name of Jesus.

I command destructive powers in the waters to destroy my enemies, in the name of Jesus. Let my enemies perish before waters. You the earth, open up and swallow my problems. You the earth, refuse to honor every evil sacrifice done against me, in the name of Jesus. Let every evil my enemies raised against my life be buried in the dust. Every power behind my problems, be buried in the earth, I command the morning to swallow my problems, in the name of Jesus. I command the night to kill all my problems. I command the atmosphere to kill every evil raised against me, in the name of Jesus.

Let all the elements join forces to destroy my enemies, in the name of Jesus. I raise Holy Ghost altar against the wicked. I raise divine altars among the entire creations to destroy my destroyers. I command every creature to rise up and fight for me, in the name of Jesus. Let bedroom, sitting room, car, office and all places on earth where evil is planned against me fight for me. I use weapons of my enemies against them. Let everything my enemies have turn against them for my sake, in the name of Jesus.

I command every environment in all creation to favor me, in the name of Jesus. Let the creatures refuse to walk against me. I command angels of God to fight from heavens for my sake, in the name of Jesus. I bring judgment against curses in my life. Let the entire creation convert every curse against me into blessings. Every star representing my problems, catch fire and burn to ashes, in the name of Jesus. I bring down every evil star against me in the heavenlies. Every power behind my problems, be arrested, in the name of Jesus.

Let the entire creation destroy every physical and spiritual organization against my life, in the name of Jesus. Let whirlwind from heaven blow off heads of the wicked. I command my personal evil stronghold to be consumed by fire. Let great earthquake locate the camp of my enemies now, in the name of Jesus. I release seaquake to waste all my destiny wasters in the waters. I command the air to quake for my sake and destroy works of evil principalities against my life. Horrible tempest, fall upon the camp of my enemies, in the name of Jesus.

Let the furnace of affliction oppress my oppressors to death, in the name of Jesus. I send brimstone and fire from heavens against my unrepentant enemies. I command madness to enter into brains of my unrepentant enemies. Fire of blindness, possess the eyes of my wicked enemies, in the name of Jesus. Let the bones of my enemies lose their strength. I feed all my oppressors with bread and water of affliction, in the name of Jesus. I command the cloud of sorrow to cover all my enemies. Let the unbearable heat from hell fire, burn my enemies, in the name of Jesus.

Let destroying flood from above sweep away my enemies, in the name of Jesus. Let shock, stroke and destruction visit the wicked for my sake. Let the wind of God take disappointments to my enemies, in the name of Jesus. Let arrows of failure be relayed to my enemies. I command evil worms to eat up all my stubborn enemies. Let all my problems face bitter destruction this year, in the name of Jesus. I send arrows of bitter destruction to all my enemies this year. Let all my stubborn enemies gather themselves to destruction, in the name of Jesus.

Whatever devil has done against my life, receive death, in the name of Jesus. Let all that agents of devil did against me die forever. Every power that will work to renew my bondage this year shall fail and perish, in the name of Jesus. I raise uncompromising wrath of God against my enemies from today. Let the earth, sun, moon and stars, refuse to answer devil and his agents for my sake. I instruct all the elements to fight back all my enemies from today, in the name of Jesus. Every evil word that will be uttered against me from today will backfire. Let the cloud, tempest, thunder, lightning, hailstone, rain, snow and the dew frustrate my enemies in the future. Let the entire creation begin to oppress my past, present and future enemies to death. I seal my prayers of authority with the seal of God forever, in the name of Jesus.

DECREE 52

Every evil power assigned to frustrate my life this year, be frustrated, in the name of Jesus. Blood of Jesus, speak peace and prosperity into my life this year. Lord, arise and prosper my handiwork this year. Every satanic investment in my life, perish. Let all my good dreams begin to manifest without hindrances this year. Every marine spirit seed planted in my life, receive fire and perish. Every leviathan working against my progress, perish. Every evil movement against my life, be demobilized. Every evil bird flying against my life, I break your wings, in the name of Jesus. Every evil planted in the heart of everyone against my life, perish. I cut every evil hand raised against my destiny, in the name of Jesus.

You my ghost of evil pasts, you will not function in my life again, in the name of Jesus. Every enemy of my peace, be wasted by thunder. Every evil voice attacking me from the grave, be silenced. Every evil arrow of death fired into my life, backfire. Every seed of immorality in my life, perish, in the name of Jesus. I command every inherited problem to die and be wasted. Every power sponsoring failure in my life, be disgraced unto death. Every voice of witchcraft shouting against my life, perish, in the name of Jesus.

Every seed of non-achievement in my life, catch fire, in the name of Jesus. Every strongman challenging my destiny, die by force. Every satanic blockage to the flow of divine miracles into my life, be cleared away, in the name of Jesus. Blood of Jesus, flow into my life and advertise Your goodness. Fire of God, enter into my life and burn to ashes every problem affecting my life. Lord, renew my life and empower me to produce great miracles. Every power attacking my glory, perish, in the name of Jesus.

Let the flushing power of God enter into my foundation now, in the name of Jesus. I bind and cast out my life every agent of poverty. Let deliverance power of God enter into my life and deliver me. Every evil force bearing evil fruits in my life, be uprooted, in the name of Jesus. Lord, increase my wisdom this year against the wisdom of devil. Father Lord, develop my skill and talent to the highest level, in the name of Jesus. Every evil deposit in my life, perish. Every power increasing my problems, perish, in the name of Jesus.

Every foundational problem that has vowed to waste my life, be wasted, in the name of Jesus. Every property of witchcraft in my life, be destroyed. Every satanic armed robber assigned to my life, perish. Fire of Holy Ghost, increase in my life by Your power. Every enemy of my promotion, perish, in the name of Jesus. Oh Lord, arise and deliver me, I command every area of my life to receive victory today, in the name of Jesus.

DECREE 53

Every agent of demonic delay in my life, wherever you are now, perish, in the name of Jesus. I command every messenger of backwardness to be frustrated in my life. Every satanic embargo planted on my way, be lifted, in the name of Jesus. Every wicked oppressor militating against my life, be oppressed. Every arrow of late progress in my life, backfire. Every weapon of failure in my life, be roasted by fire, in the name of Jesus. Every serpent of darkness vomiting fire into my life, die by your fire. Every evil leg that had walked into my life, walk out by force, in the name of Jesus.

Every agent of death assigned to kill me, kill your sender and perish, in the name of Jesus. Let all spiritual armed robbers begin to rob all my enemies. Every evil signboard mounted against me, be uprooted. Every evil tree bearing evil fruits against me, be uprooted, in the name of Jesus. I break and loose myself from inherited bondages. Every sickness in my life that wants to accompany me to the grave, perish, in the name of Jesus. Every satanic chain tying my blessings, break by force. Every problem attached to my name, be detached by force, in the name of Jesus.

Blood of Jesus, speak me out of every bondage, in the name of Jesus. Every evil king sitting upon my life, be unseated by death. Every enemy of my breakthrough, perish, in the name of Jesus. Lord, arise and take me to my place of deliverance. Every wicked voice crying in my life, be silenced to death. Every instrument of devil in my life, be roasted by fire, in the name of Jesus. I command every evil gang-up against my life to scatter. I receive keys to open doors to greatness, in the name of Jesus.

Every witchcraft power working hard to disgrace my life, be disgraced, in the name of Jesus. Every organ of my life under attack, be delivered by force. I receive supernatural anointing to overcome every problem in my life, in the name of Jesus. Every evil program going on against my life, be terminated. Every witchcraft broom sweeping away my blessings, burn to ashes. Every danger ahead of my life this year, disappear in shame, in the name of Jesus. Every power commissioned to frustrate my destiny, be frustrated. Every evil veil covering my glory, catch fire and burn to ashes, in the name of Jesus.

Every satanic satellite monitoring my life, be blinded forever, in the name of Jesus. Lord, remove Everything on earth sheltering my enemies from judgment. Let God arise and remove hedge of protection from my strongman. Every evil spirit that has captured my destiny, be cast out and be disgraced, in the name of Jesus. I command the strength of enduring problems in my life to fail, I walk every demon out of my life. Let every satanic joy over my life be converted to tears, in the name of Jesus.

DECREE 54

Every book devil has written against my life, catch fire and burn to ashes, in the name of Jesus. Every witchcraft bird eating up my glory, vomit them and perish. Every agent of poverty in my life, perish. Every man or woman sitting on my benefits, rights and entitlement, be unseated by fire, in the name of Jesus. Every organized darkness working hard to disgrace me, be disgraced. Father Lord, empower me to destroy every demonic activity, in Jesus name. Every darkness in the throne of my life, disappear by force, in the name of Jesus.

Every agent of shame in my life, be frustrated shamefully, in the name of Jesus. Every satanic network against my life, scatter by force. I reject every invitation to immorality, in the name of Jesus. I command the joy of my oppressors to disappear. Every invisible bondage in my life, break, in the name of Jesus. Lord, give me an understanding that will take me to another level. Every evil judgment passed upon my life, be reversed, in the name of Jesus. I command all my captured blessings to be released by force. I move into the universe with Holy Ghost wind against my enemies, in the name of Jesus.

Lord, arise and catapult me to the top. I command every underdeveloped area of my life to receive deliverance, in the name of Jesus. Every evil force blocking my heavens, be cleared away by thunder. Lord Jesus, kill every evil appetite assigned to disgrace me. Every good thing I have lost in life, I recover you double, in the name of Jesus. Every ancestral pollution in my life, be cleansed by the blood of Jesus. Every witchcraft plantation in my life, be uprooted. Every satanic river flowing into my life, dry up now, in the name of Jesus.

Every evil hand stealing from my destiny, wither by force, in the name of Jesus. Every enemy in my bedroom, perish. Every evil investment of my parents, catch the Holy Ghost fire. Every marriage in the spirit troubling my life, break by force, in the name of Jesus. Every evil meal I have eating in my dream, I vomit you out by force. I break and loose myself from the hold of evil powers. Every stranger in my body, you are finished, come out and perish, in the name of Jesus. Let every territorial problem assigned to waste my destiny be wasted. Every negative thing living in my body, be removed by fire, the name of Jesus.

Let strange fire burning in my life be quenched by force, in the name of Jesus. You my destiny, move from bondage to liberty now. Every evil covenant assigned to disgrace me, break. Every conscious and unconscious utterance I have ever made that is now troubling my life, perish. I withdraw my destiny from evil captivities, in the name of Jesus. I take authority over every problem in my life. Every good thing in my life that is under a curse, be delivered, in the name of Jesus.

DECREE 55

I discharge every area of my life from captivity of demonic spirits, in the name of Jesus. Every unrepentant witchcraft against my life, be disgraced. Every evil personality diverting good things from my life, be paralyzed, Every wall of security around my enemies, collapse by thunder, in the name of Jesus. Let resurrection power of God quicken everything in me that is good. I cast out every serpentine spirit delegated to attack my life. Every provision that God has made available for me this year, I receive you, in the name of Jesus.

Let the healing power of God heal every area of my life, in the name of Jesus. Blood of Jesus, flow into my life and destroy every satanic work. Holy Ghost fire, burn to ashes every problem in my life, in the name of Jesus. Every evil power waiting to destroy my efforts in life, be destroyed. Every wicked and evil priest ministering against my life, perish. I break and loose myself from captivity of Every evil altar, in the name of Jesus.

Father Lord, empower me to succeed this year, in the name of Jesus. Lord, release money into my account on earth from heavenly bank. Let every enemy of my financial breakthrough, be disgraced. Every power that is standing against my promotion, be disgraced, in the name of Jesus. I use the blood of Jesus against every evil sacrifice in my life. I command the heavenly bank to open and release all my finances. I receive power to operate as king on earth, in the name of Jesus.

Let my glory that is stolen by evil powers be released, in the name of Jesus. Every inherited poverty in my life, be dismantled by force. Holy Ghost fire, overturn every evil document filed against me, in the name of Jesus. Everything my ancestors have done with evil powers that are now troubling me, perish. Lord Jesus, arise in your power and enlarge my coast this year, in the name of Jesus. Every problem of sorrow fired into my life; I fire you back. Every evil power sitting on my greatness, be unseated by force, in the name of Jesus.

Every evil utterance ever said against my life, be converted to my favor, in the name of Jesus. Let my deliverance begin to manifest by fire. Lord, arise and silence my Goliath by death. I withdraw every inch of my life from evil kingdom, in the name of Jesus. I command the power of suffering to abandon my life this year. Let angels of the living God begin to minister deliverance unto me. Every evil flood moving to my side, be diverted by force, in the name of Jesus.

Every enemy of my joy, you are wicked, perish. Let my marriage move forward this year, in the name of Jesus. Every power standing against my moving forward, perish, in the name of Jesus. I release my greatness from witchcraft arrests. Every power assigned to activate poverty in my life, perish. Every hidden devourer in my life, devour yourself now, in the name of Jesus.

DECREE 56

Every power fighting my marriage from my place of birth, perish, in the name of Jesus. I withdraw my destiny from control of household enemies. Every evil fire burning against my life, quench. I command all my problems to begin to wither, in the name of Jesus. Let the resurrection power begin to quicken dead areas of my life this year. Every power that wants me to suffer alone while others enjoy, perish, in the name of Jesus. I command my enemies to enter into traps they have set for me. Let progresses of my wicked enemies be transferred to me, in the name of Jesus.

I command all my stubborn enemies to receive shame and disgrace, in the name of Jesus. Every vagabond spirit assigned to possess me, be frustrated. Every inner heat from the kingdom of darkness in my life, be destroyed. Every arrow of confusion fired against my life, I fire you back, in the name of Jesus. Lord, deliver me from the curse of non-achievement. Every invisible force from devil following me about, be frustrated, in the name of Jesus.

Every corruption in my reproductive organ, be corrected. Let my deliverance receive immediate results today. Every evil personality empowered to kill me, kill your sender. I command every organ of my body to receive deliverance, in the name of Jesus. Every evil arrow fired into my foundation; I pull you out. Let my frustration be frustrated to death. Every evil power that has booked me for evil, die in shame, in the name of Jesus. I withdraw my name from all evil records. Blood of Jesus, terminate every evil program going on against me, in the name of Jesus.

Every power attacking my brain, be wasted by fire, in the name of Jesus. Father Lord, command my elevation to come from you, I refuse to accept every gift of blessing from devil, in the name of Jesus. Let my marriage be singled out for blessing this year. Every power denying me of my rights, you are wicked, perish. Every strange movement in my body, be terminated, in the name of Jesus. Every agent of lack in my life, perish. Blood of Jesus, speak me out of shameful debts, in the name of Jesus.

Every power that wants to reduce me to a beggar, be frustrated, in the name of Jesus. I receive divine grace to manifest this year to the glory of God. Every evil movement designed to kill me, kill your senders this year. Every evil group that had vowed to finish me on earth, scatter in disgrace, in the name of Jesus. I restore my glory that was stolen by household wicked enemies. I cover the totality of my life with precious blood of Jesus. Every evil veil covering my greatness, catch fire, in the name of Jesus.

Let my true person begin to manifest, I shall arise and stand out above others everywhere I go this year. Every demonic agent that has vowed to deal with me, be wasted, in the name of Jesus.

DECREE 57

Every evil consultation against my destiny, begin to favor me, in the name of Jesus. I blind eyes of all evil priests ministering against my life. The legs that took my enemies into evil places because of me shall break. Every evil sacrifice offered against my life shall waste my enemies. Every evil umbrella covering my life, I tear you into pieces, in the name of Jesus. Let my stolen blessings be restored back to me. Every hand that will carry evil against my life shall break. Let destructive stroke visit my stubborn enemies, in the name of Jesus.

Every evil mouth that will open against me shall remain open to their shame, in the name of Jesus. Every invitation I gave to devil in the past, I withdraw you. Every witchcraft or wizard rejoicing over my life, begin to cry. Father Lord, begin to disengage all my enemies from their evil works, in the name of Jesus. Lord, plant your gifts and talents in the garden of my life. Every evil book containing evil assignment against my life, catch fire, in the name of Jesus.

You my life, escape from evil captivities forever, in the name of Jesus. Every power that wants to bring me back to a lower level, perish. Every evil garment upon my life, catch fire. Holy Ghost fire, born to ashes every garment of suffering in my life. Every problem assigned to take me to the grave, take my enemy there, in the name of Jesus. I reject every evil visitor that is coming from the waters. Every evil agreement everywhere against me, scatter. Lord, change my garment to your glory this year. I refuse to bow to every problem, problems must bow to me, in the name of Jesus.

Every power assigned to make me a fool, be fooled before you come, in the name of Jesus. Let the backbone of my unrepentant Goliath be broken. I dry up all the waters in the containers of my enemies with fire. Let my enemies begin to imagine evil against themselves, in the name of Jesus. Power to stop my enemy's programs, possess me now. Lord, arise and pull me out of destruction, in the name of Jesus. Every bad dream prepared against my life this year, die in the spirit. Every evil personality bringing back affliction into my life, die with it, in the name of Jesus.

You the architect of evil designs in my life, I cut off your head, in the name of Jesus. Every satanic back door into my life, be closed forever. Every witchcraft weapon against my life, catch fire and burn to ashes, in the name of Jesus. I receive my own portion of blessing this very year. You the tragedy that will expose my enemies, what are you waiting for? Manifest now. My finances presently in the hands of devil, I withdraw you now, in the name of Jesus.

Every power that wants me to go round the circle again this year, perish, in the name of Jesus. I employ services of God's angels to open doors of blessings to me. I receive power to make great progress in my life this year, in the name of Jesus. Every evil gathering against my life this year, scatter. Every hinderance to my advancement, be scattered by thunder, in the name of Jesus. Lord, give me the secret of breakthrough that cannot fail me this year. I walk every enemy of my promotion to their doom this year. Every evil list containing my name, receive fire and burn to ashes, in the name of Jesus.

DECREE 58

Every weapon of destruction being used against me, be destroyed, in the name of Jesus. Let brains of all my stubborn enemies receive faults. I release fire of God into the camp of my enemies. Let all my buried blessings be exhumed. Every witchcraft mark in Every part of my body, be blotted by blood of Jesus, in the name of Jesus. Every witch or wizard searching for my destiny, receive madness. Every curse of manipulation in my life, expire by fire. Every spiritual locust eating up my life, be roasted by fire, in the name of Jesus.

I command my star to escape from every evil prison now, in the name of Jesus. Every power assigned to take me back to square one, be frustrated. Every inherited embargo, I reject you. Every power spoiling my efforts, perish, in the name of Jesus. Father Lord, lead me to my place of rest and peace. I break and loose myself from yoke of sudden death, in the name of Jesus. I command every root of bitterness in my life to be converted to joy. Lord, arise and take over the management of my home. Every power of evil desolation walking into my home, perish, in the name of Jesus.

Every mistake prepared to ruin my life, I avoid you forever, in the name of Jesus. Every evil power preventing my glory from manifesting, perish. I command every evil inheritance in my life to be disowned. Father Lord, convert my frustration to fulfillment today. Every messenger of disgrace approaching my life, take it back to your sender. Power to disgrace my disgrace, possess me now, in the name of Jesus. Every property of devil in my life, be roasted by fire. Father Lord, create rooms for more blessings in my life this year, in the name of Jesus.

Every serpent of darkness in my life, perish, in the name of Jesus. Let my blood reject every sickness and disease flowing inside it now. Let every habitation of the wicked in my life be disgraced out. Every power contending with my glory, you are wicked; perish, in the name of Jesus. Every strange action taking place in my life, be terminated. Every evil bird crying against my destiny, be silenced. Lord, arise and take me to your original plan for my life, in the name of Jesus.

DECREE 59

I receive power to accept divine counsel that will lead me to greatness, in the name of Jesus. Every arrow of depression fired into my destiny, backfire. Arrows of unexplainable problem in my life, come out now. Anointing of rising and falling in my life, break by fire, in the name of Jesus. I break and loose myself from uncontrollable sexual desires. Every power responsible for financial problems in my life, perish, in the name of Jesus. Serpent in charge of deep-rooted evil habits in my life, perish. Every agent of intimidation and fear in my life, be disgraced, in the name of Jesus.

Every agent of demonic lateness in my life, be frustrated, in the name of Jesus. Every determined enemy in my place of work, be fired. Every part of my destiny inside the waters, come out now, in the name of Jesus. Every good thing I have lost to water spirits, I recover you double. Every known or unknown person having sex with me in the spirit, perish, in the name of Jesus. I command the powers attacking my memory to be wasted. Father Lord, lead me to take good decisions on time, in the name of Jesus. Every power causing me to make mistakes over and over, perish. Every power destroying my lifetime investment, perish, in the name of Jesus.

I recover every good opportunity I have ever lost in life, in the name of Jesus. I break and loose myself from every yoke of restlessness. Lord, arise and promote me spiritually. I walk out from all places I have ever been to for good, in the name of Jesus. Every power that has captured my life in my old school, city, etc., release me by force. I put off every old uniform. Every spirit of carry-over in my life, fall down and perish, in the name of Jesus. I receive power to start Every good thing and finish it on time. I pursue all my pursuers in my dreams, in the name of Jesus.

Every agent of blockage at the edge of my miracle, perish, in the name of Jesus. I refuse to record Every failure again in my lifetime. I break and loose myself from the grip of incurable sickness, in the name of Jesus. Every power attacking my sleep, perish. Every power assigned to interrupt my joy and progress, be destroyed. Every mark of hatred and rejection in my life, disappear. From this year, I refuse to meet wrong people in life. Father Lord, link me up with true helpers who will be able to help me, in the name of Jesus. I command people around me to love and care for me, in the name of Jesus. Lord, increase my friends and reduce my enemies, in the name of Jesus.

DECREE 60

Every power making prayers difficult for me, perish, in the name of Jesus. Every power making easy things difficult, your time is up, perish. Every power making difficult things impossible for me, disappear and perish. Every power of impossibilities in my life, be wasted. I refuse to fight my divinely ordained helpers, in the name of Jesus. Lord, help me to reduce my battles of life to zero point. I command every part of my being never to forsake God. The blood my ancestors shed that is now crying against my life, be silenced by the blood of Jesus. Every wicked plan of devil and his agents against me this year, perish, in the name of Jesus.

Every minister of problem designed to disgrace me, be disgraced, in the name of Jesus. Every arrow of demonic lusts in my life, backfire. Every witchcraft manipulation going on against my life, expire, I command every serpent of excessive anger in my life to perish, in the name of Jesus. Let all foundational problems in my life perish, I break and loose myself from every evil initiation, I refuse to respond to every evil summon from now and forever. I frustrate every demonic prayer team raised against my life. I walk out from the captivity of every bewitchment, in the name of Jesus.

Every water spirit poison circulating inside my body, be purged, in the name of Jesus. Let every spiritual armed robber that visits me perish. I break the backbone of all ancestral powers against me. Let all my envious enemies begin to waste themselves, I break and loose myself from powers of wrong choices. Every property of the grave and death in my life, catch fire, in the name of Jesus. Every yoke of iniquity in my life break by force. Let every arrow of marine powers in my life disappear. I reject every evil dedication troubling my life, in the name of Jesus.

Every power diverting good things away from my life, perish, in the name of Jesus. Lord, expose and disgrace every unfriendly friend against me. I refuse to be drunk with evil and every kind of problem. Every serpent of sexual sin in my life, die by fire, in the name of Jesus. Every place that has become a cage for my life, I walk away from you. Every weapon of paralysis in my life, be roasted by fire. I bring back every good thing devil has removed from me. Every messenger of demotion in my life, be demoted, in the name of Jesus. Wherever my destiny is locked up, I release it now. I command every hindrance in my life to disappear forever, in the name of Jesus.

DECREE 61

Every area of my life that the enemy has arrested, I command your release now, in the name of Jesus. Every power hindering my financial breakthrough, I command you to give way. You my demoted destiny, receive promotion from above now, in the name of Jesus. Every wicked power that has vowed to frustrate my life, be frustrated. Lord, arise and make me more dangerous than the most dangerous evil, I command the resurrection power of God to quicken my executed destiny, in the name of Jesus.

Every great blessing that the enemy has stolen from me, be recovered, in the name of Jesus. Every judgment passed against my life, be reversed to my favor. Lord, arise and erase curses in my life. Let divine movement begin to move my life away from stagnation. Every good thing devil has stopped me from given birth to, be delivered now, in the name of Jesus. Father Lord, command my oppressors to be arrested. Every power molesting my destiny, be disgraced publicly, in the name of Jesus.

You my determined household Cain, kill yourself by mistake, in the name of Jesus. Every power that wants me to die under the flood of judgment, perish. I refuse to die childless, both spiritual and physical, in the name of Jesus. Every spiritual Sodom and Gomorrah raised against me; I escape your evil. My source of provision will never dry up, whether devil likes it or not. I command my spiritual eyes to open to see divine provisions, in the name of Jesus.

I command all manner of lack in my life to perish, in the name of Jesus. The well of my life will never dry up, in Jesus name. Every problem forcing me to sell my birthright, be terminated. Let every yoke of slavery in my life break this year, in the name of Jesus. Every power delaying divine visitation in my life, give way. Every spirit of fear tormenting my destiny, disappear now, in the name of Jesus. Every serpent in my father's house eating up my favor, die this year. Lord, use this prayers to change my name this year, in the name of Jesus.

Every power that wants me to get rotten in one level of life, perish, in the name of Jesus. I break and loose myself from my Egyptian bondage. Every arrow of confusion about to destroy my life, disappear, in the name of Jesus. The plague that is wasting others shall not come near me forever. I convert the success of my enemies into disgraceful failures. Let my eagle arise, fly and reach the goal and destination of my life, in the name of Jesus. I receive boldness to intimidate all my oppressors. Every satanic army raised against my life, scatter in shame. Every area of my life lacking the water of life, be watered to overflow, in the name of Jesus.

DECREE 62

Every evil group living in my promise land, scatter and be displaced, in the name of Jesus. Every area of my life under demonic oppression, be released by force. I receive back all that I have lost to my enemies in the past. Father Lord, show me the fullness of your glory this year, in the name of Jesus. Every demonic leprosy in my life, visible or invisible, be cleansed. I command my prayer altar to receive fire. Every evil tongue in my family speaking against my life, close by fire, in the name of Jesus.

I walk out from Every pestilence destroying my area, in the name of Jesus. Every evil voice speaking continuously against my destiny, be silenced. Every evil sacrifice crying against my life, cry no more. Every rebellion raised against me from everywhere, be disgraced, in the name of Jesus. I walk into my promised land and I possess my possession. I command my destiny to reject every curse placed upon it. Let the voice of resurrection command my destiny out of every grave, in the name of Jesus.

Father Lord, breathe Your life into my life now, in the name of Jesus. Every instrument of death ready to kill me, kill your owner. Lord, command Your grace to increase in my life. Every evil personality ready to put me into trouble, be exposed, in the name of Jesus. Lord, arise in Your power and quench my thirsts, I drink from the well of waters of life. Every Delilah or strange woman that has vowed to waste my life, perish, in the name of Jesus. Lord, pour Your anointing oil on my head and bless me. Every power preventing me from hearing God's Voice, perish, in the name of Jesus.

Every occultic demand in my life, I reject you by force, in the name of Jesus. Every power sharing my property while I am still alive, perish. Every power preventing me from hearing God's Word, perish. I remove every wicked personality sitting upon my destiny. I hit the four head of my Goliath to death by force, I receive power to use my life to glorify God all the days of my life, in the name of Jesus. Every power that wants to blind me, fail woefully and be blinded. I destroy every plan of the stranger woman against my destiny, in the name of Jesus.

Father Lord, feed me with the food of the champion, in the name of Jesus. Every evil prophecy against my life, be aborted. Let the witchcraft of Every Jezebel kill her and her children, in the name of Jesus. I receive the gift of Holy Ghost to raise the dead. Every witchcraft threat against my life, be nullified, in the name of Jesus.

DECREE 63

Lord, use these prayers to change my destiny for good this year, in the name of Jesus. Let angels of the living God invade my enemy's camp for my sake. Let my remaining enemies in the battle field perish. Lord, pour Your power into my life as never before, in the name of Jesus. I command my foundation to vomit every evil planted in it. I receive power to begin all that I suppose to begin. Every power of poor finishing in my life, perish, in the name of Jesus. Father Lord, arise and bless the works of my hands. Every evil altar working against my destiny, scatter. Power to start well and end well to the glory of God, possess me, in the name of Jesus.

Every seed of defeat planted in my life, perish, in the name of Jesus. Every enemy of new project in my life, perish. Every power from the waters that wants to control my life, perish. Every evil power pursuing me up and down, be pursued unto death. Every evil sacrifice boasting against my life, be silenced by the blood of Jesus. Let the voice of the enemy speaking against my life perish. Power of God, destroy every circle of hardship in my life. Every destructive voice crying against my prosperity, perish, in the name of Jesus.

Every evil material polluting my mind, be destroyed, in the name of Jesus. You my family idol on assignment to destroy my life, be destroyed. Every arrow of disgrace fired against my life, backfire. Every serpent assigned to swallow my present efforts, perish, in the name of Jesus. Let witchcraft attacks fighting against my life be disgraced. Holy Ghost fire, burn to ashes every demonic property in my life, in the name of Jesus. Let every terror of the night looking for my greatness perish. Father Lord, arise and terrorize my terrors, in the name of Jesus.

Every evil unity organized to waste my destiny, be wasted, in the name of Jesus. I scatter every evil organization working hard to destroy my life. Every demonic gang-up against my life, die by fire. I command all my strong enemies to be put to shame. Every power on assignment to waste my life, be wasted, in the name of Jesus. I cast out every invisible power chasing me all around. Father Lord, scatter every evil cloud gathering against my destiny. Every evil mouth mocking me, I mock you to death, in the name of Jesus.

Every evil mouth opened to drink my blood, drink poison and perish, in the name of Jesus. I render null and void every evil decision taken against me. I decree my name too hot to be controlled by the devil, in the name of Jesus.

DECREE 64

Every good thing I have ever lost, I recover you double, in the name of Jesus. Every witchcraft threat to my life, I command you to fail. I command every evil counsel against my life to be turned to foolishness. I receive power to overcome every evil advance from evil women. Every evil plantation in my life from graveyard, perish, in the name of Jesus. I reject every reproach assigned to blaspheme God in my life. Every arrow of untimely death fired against my destiny, perish, in the name of Jesus.

Let every demonic effort against my life fail woefully, in the name of Jesus. I command every evil visitor in my family to be destroyed. Every evil personality compelling me to compromise evil, perish. I refuse to suffer under the debt of my old parents, in the name of Jesus. Let heads of all my stubborn enemies be removed by force. Every storm gathering against my life, scatter in shame. Every yoke of sin holding me down, break. Let every tree of failure planted in my life be uprooted, in the name of Jesus.

Every seed of wickedness planted in my life, die by fire, in the name of Jesus. Every enemy of my greatness, collapse by thunder. Fire of God, burn to ashes every evil fire burning in my life, in the name of Jesus.

DECREE 65

Every handwriting of my family's strongman against my life, catch fire, in the name of Jesus. I bring and cast out every devourer of my destiny. I break and loose myself from every inherited covenant. Blood of Jesus, speak my destiny out of every captivity, in the name of Jesus. I cancel every course of inherited poverty in my life, in the name of Jesus. Let my household wickedness be exposed unto destruction. Every enemy of my greatness. I command fire to burn you, in the name of Jesus. Every curse of infirmity in my life, expire by fire. I break and loose myself from all manners of generational captivity, in the name of Jesus.

Every defeat I have ever suffered in the dream, be converted to victory, in the name of Jesus. Every evil leg that is walking inside my life, begin to walk out. Let all satanic progresses in my life be arrested by fire, in the name of Jesus. Every evil personality that has swallowed my prosperity, vomit them by force. I purge evil consumptions out of my life. Arrows of serpentine kingdom in my life, come out, in the name of Jesus. Every hard problem in my life, die by force. Let the stronghold of my problem collapse, in the name of Jesus.

DECREE 66

Every evil river advertising my defeat, dry up by fire, in the name of Jesus. Every agent of oppression in my life, be disgraced. Let all my benefits stolen by household enemies be recovered. Let this prayer program arrest every enemy of my destiny. You the spirit of failure in my life, be beheaded, in the name of Jesus. Powers of desert spirits working against my life, be squeezed to death. Every evil hand raised against my destiny, I cut you off. Every imported demon that has vowed to lead me to my grave, die alone. Every demon behind evil covenants in my life, be arrested, in the name of Jesus.

Agents of marital demotion working against my life, perish, in the name of Jesus. I break and loose myself from captivity of the strongman. Every evil summons designed to waste my efforts in life, fail. I walk out from all evil parental designs, in the name of Jesus. I refuse to answer Every call from the kingdom of darkness. Every wicked leader placed above me, be disgraced. Let every demonic breeze directed against me be diverted, in the name of Jesus. Every evil voice attacking me from the grave, be silenced. Let enemies of my prosperity be arrested to death, in the name of Jesus.

DECREE 67

Every satanic property in my house, I burn you to ashes, in the name of Jesus. Lord Jesus, deliver me from the hands of wicked elders. Every satanic judge sitting down to judge me, receive stroke. Every power assigned to redesign the map of my destiny, perish, in the name of Jesus. I frustrate all my foes and I command them to prostrate to me. Let the hand of God begin to plant miracles into my life. Every handwriting of lack in my life, be rubbed off by blood of Jesus, in the name of Jesus. Every demonic poison circulating in my body, dry up. I command the bank of heaven to release money into my account this year, in the name of Jesus.

I receive unmerited favor from heaven by God's grace, in the name of Jesus. God, protect every ground I have recovered from the enemy. Every evil chain dragging me away from God, break. God, arise and fight my battles to the end, in the name of Jesus. Every evil altar militating against my destiny, be uprooted. I command my glory to escape from captivity of evil actors. Let deep rooted problems in my life be wasted. Lord, take me to Your place of victory this year. Every evil done against my life from the womb, expire, in the name of Jesus.

DECREE 68

I paralyze every agent of shame working against me this year, in the name of Jesus. I receive divine wisdom that will make me great this year. Every seed of unfruitfulness planted in my life, perish, in the name of Jesus. Let my voice prevail over voice of witchcraft this year. I receive divine direction to walk according to God's will this year. Father Lord, frustrate every device of devil in my life this year. Every evil decree working against my destiny, be revoked, in the name of Jesus. I command failures to be frustrated out of my life forever. Lord, protect me and my family from satanic destructions, in the name of Jesus.

I receive the anointing to overcome every witchcraft attack, in the name of Jesus. I repair and restore damages done to my life through witchcraft attacks. Every satanic agent assigned to waste my destiny, fail woefully. Every curse placed upon my life from my mother's womb, expire. I release burning fire of God against my stubborn enemies, in the name of Jesus. I reject every invitation or summon from the occultic world. Every evil gift devil is using to entice me, I reject you. I command evil and wicked plans against my life to fail. I receive the anointing to break every evil yoke in my life, in the name of Jesus.

Blood of Jesus, flow into my life and deliver me today, in the name of Jesus. I command every seed of curse in my life to perish, I close up every pothole in my businesses by fire. Every satanic building standing against my life, catch fire, in the name of Jesus. Every satanic caterpillar destroying good things in my life, perish. Every satanic agent planning to terminate my life, kill yourself, in the name of Jesus. Every arrow of witchcraft fired into my destiny, backfire. Every strange woman empowered to confuse me, be frustrated, in the name of Jesus.

Every power that wants me to regret for doing right things, perish, in the name of Jesus. Every demon that has captured my reasoning, release me by force. I recover every good thing my ancestors lost to idols. Every power misdirecting my love, I paralyze your efforts, in the name of Jesus. Every evil voice calling me into sin, be silenced forever. I break and loose myself from Every secret relationship. I bind and cast out every spirit of immorality from my life forever, in the name of Jesus. Every work of occultic agents calling me to disobey God, perish. Every evil power keeping me away from God's blessings, release me and perish, in the name of Jesus.

Every satanic bondage keeping me out of God's blessings, break, in the name of Jesus. I command every evil movement against my life to stop. I break and loose myself from every evil chain, in the name of Jesus.

DECREE 69

I Command every problem that is stronger than me to perish before Christ, in the name of Jesus. Every stubborn infirmity destroying people in every neighborhood, be wasted. I break and lose myself from wicked household enemies. Every destructive problem standing against my life, receive destruction, in the name of Jesus. Let every consistent demonic attack against my life perish. Every evil flow from my ancestors into my life, dry up by fire, in the name of Jesus.

Every inherited yoke in my life, break to pieces, in the name of Jesus. I pour blood of Jesus into the root of my life. Every demonic serpent attacking my destiny, die without mercy, in the name of Jesus. Every concrete problem in my life, receive death. Every stubborn problem in my blood, be purged, in the name of Jesus. Ancient of days, arise and restore my destiny to its original blueprint. Let every enemy of my comfort die wherever they are, in the name of Jesus.

I command every good thing I have ever lost to be recovered, in the name of Jesus. Father Lord, keep me perfectly in Your plan everyday. Every effect of curses in my life, be roasted by fire. Every root of inherited immorality in my life, be uprooted, in the name of Jesus. I command every voice of evil in my life to be silenced by blood of Jesus. Every satanic cobweb designed to disgrace me, be burnt to ashes. Every enchantment of the wicked against my life, perish, in the name of Jesus.

Every enemy of my freedom, you are finished, perish, in the name of Jesus. Lord, arise and deliver me by fire. Every defeat I have ever suffered in life, be converted to victory, in the name of Jesus. Every enemy in the battlefield against my life, receive confusion. Every power causing me to lust or seek after a witch or wizard, perish. I break and loose myself from doing another man's job. Father Lord, engage me only in the assignment You gave me, in the name of Jesus.

Every false spirit within and around me, I cast you out, in the name of Jesus. Father Lord, make all crooked ways of my life to become straight. Lord, help me to destroy every evil foundation to build new ones. I command evil oppressions in my life to stop by force, in the name of Jesus. I pull down every strongman in the throne of my life. I remove all my blessings from the camp of darkness. I command all my spiritual enemies to be arrested, in the name of Jesus. Every evil plantation that is about to grow in my life, be uprooted, in the name of Jesus.

Blood of Jesus, begin to cleanse my foundation, in the name of Jesus. Every waster of my destiny, I waste you now. Every seed of shame and reproach in my life, die by hot fire, in the name of Jesus. Every activity of witchcraft against my life, be terminated. Every evil gate opened by my enemies, close forever, in the name of Jesus. Every satanic full stop in my life, be removed by force, in the name of Jesus. Let fire of God chase away every serpent in the garden of my life, in the name of Jesus. Every part of my destiny that is lost, I recover you, in the name of Jesus.

I pull out my star from the hands of oppressors, in the name of Jesus.

I release all my captured progresses from the captivity of devil, in the name of Jesus. I break the backbone of my family strongman. Every part of my life that is naked, spiritual or physical, be covered now, in the name of Jesus. Every spiritual mark of hatred and rejection in my life, be destroyed. Every door of opportunity locked against my life, open by force, I receive power of God to face all the battles of my life, in the name of Jesus. I command all my destiny helpers to appear and help me, I command every sorrow in my life to be converted to joy, in the name of Jesus.

Father Lord, return me back to my rightful place in life, in the name of Jesus. Every evil personality diverting my greatness and blessing, die without mercy. I command Every spirit assigned to destroy my marriage to be destroyed. Lord Jesus, move me from the wrong places to the rightful place in life, in the name of Jesus. I recover all my lost hopes in life. You my life, move from poverty to greatness this year. I take back every good thing my ancestors handed over to devil, I pull down every stronghold of devil that is confronting my life, in the name of Jesus.

Every evil assignment about to be accomplish in my life, perish, in the name of Jesus. Let divine forces move me from tail region to mountain top. Let every evil spirit in my life be ejected by fire, in the name of Jesus. I receive power to live life above devil all the time. Every evil personality coming to me in my dream, I overcome you. I take full charge over my life from evil forces from today. I command my entire problems to receive death verdict and perish, in the name of Jesus. I command the nature of Adam to die in my life. Every invisible chain of bondage in my life, break, in the name of Jesus.

I recover all my lost potentials. Let the hands of evil ones upon my life be cut off this year, in the name of Jesus. I command my life to rise up from where the enemy has kept it. I command my life to begin to rebel against every dark power. I reject every demotion and accept divine promotions, in the name of Jesus. I command all my stolen virtues to be recovered this year. Every demonic influence in my life, be removed by force. Every negative hindrance in my life, be hindered by force, in the name of Jesus. You the light of my destiny, be rekindled by force. Every demonic stagnation in my life, be removed by force, in the name of Jesus. Every part of my life that has expired, be renewed. I command every weakness in my life to be replaced with strength, in the name of Jesus.

DECREE 70

You the detained eagle of my life, be released by force, in the name of Jesus. I command all my blessings that are scattered to be gathered together. Every part of my life that is condemned, receive freedom. Every dead organ in my body, receive abundant life, in the name of Jesus. From this year, I will begin to harvest my labors with joy. Every satanic spell and manipulation going on against my life, I stop you, in the name of Jesus. Every arrow of premature death in my life, be replaced with long life, in the name of Jesus. I command every evil desire in my life to be converted to good desires. Every agent of backwardness in my life, be wasted, in the name of Jesus.

I receive perfect victory over periodical problems in my life, in the name of Jesus. I loose myself from the bands of the wicked by fire. I terminate the ministry of hardship and suffering in my life. I bring God's fullness of light into every dark area of my life, in the name of Jesus. Father Lord, appear in the battlefield of my life and give me victory. Every power keeping me below God's plan for my life, release me and perish, in the name of Jesus. Every power forcing me to look back to my Sodom, I cut off your existence. I break and loose myself from torments of my past sexual sins, in the name of Jesus.

I recover my lost glory and birthrights by fire, in the name of Jesus. Every strange attack going on in my life, be terminated. Lord, forgive me and deliver me from Your rebukes and plagues, in the name of Jesus. Every enemy that is enjoying my defeat, be defeated unto death. Every serpentine venom in my life, dry up, in the name of Jesus. Every spoiler of my life, be spoilt, Father Lord, empower me to recover my lost position in life. Lord, deliver me from Every divine judgment You placed upon me, in the name of Jesus.

I break and loose myself from every demonic pestilence, in the name of Jesus. Every power increasing the number of my enemies, reduce them and perish. Every evil occurrence in my family, I separate myself from you. Every power that wants to bring back all problems my parents went through into my life, perish, in the name of Jesus. Every yoke of incurable disease and impossibilities in my life, break. Every problem in my life from pit of hell, be terminated, in the name of Jesus.

Every area of my life about to experience failure, receive divine visitation, in the name of Jesus. I refuse to live my life under the mercy of devil. Every satanic doom about to operate fully in my life, be destroyed. I walk out of poverty, drought and debts, in the name of Jesus. Every grave danger ahead of my life, be removed far from me. All my wages in the hand of my oppressors, I recover you double, in the name of Jesus. Every yoke of ignorance in my life, break, in the name of Jesus.

DECREE 71

Every evil device placed upon my way to control my destiny, be removed, in the name of Jesus. Owners of evil load in my life, appear and carry your loads. Every evil load hanging in every part of my life, drop by force. I break and loose myself from every evil coalition, in the name of Jesus. I break and loose myself from generational captivity. Every agent of oppression in my life, be oppressed. I command every yoke of slavery in my life to break, in the name of Jesus. Let every environmental yoke of darkness in my life break. Let every evil burden in my life begin to fall off, in the name of Jesus.

Every worrisome situation in my life, disappear, in the name of Jesus. Every evil personality constituting problems in my life, be disgraced. Every restriction placed upon my progress, be removed, in the name of Jesus. I command every wicked plot to reduce my divine growth to be destroyed. I break and loose myself from perpetual bondages, in the name of Jesus. Every demonic family interference in my destiny, be frustrated. Every power corrupting my destiny, be arrested to death. Every area of my life being manipulated by every strange person, be delivered, in the name of Jesus.

Lord, arise and deliver me form all influences of ungodly people, in the name of Jesus. Every covenant with spirit wife or husband in my life, consciously or unconsciously, break. Every dark spirit moving in every part of my life, I cast you out. Every water spirit attacking my life, attack yourself and perish, in the name of Jesus. Every power that wants me to end my journey on earth without God, perish. Every blessing designed to rob me of my honor, I reject you, in the name of Jesus.

Every agent of devil assigned to destroy my integrity, be wasted, in the name of Jesus. I reject Everything empowered to cause my riches to disappear. Every prosperity that is not from God, I reject you, in the name of Jesus. Everything in my life pushing God far away from me, perish. Every prosperity designed to waste my life, I reject you, be wasted. Lord, command my labors to profit me greatly, in the name of Jesus. Every power assigned to return me to poverty level, die without mercy. I reject everything in place assigned to make my name to rot, in the name of Jesus.

Every blessing filled with sorrow, I reject you forever, in the name of Jesus. Everything in my life that does not have God's approval, disappear. Lord, reduce the strength of all my enemies and increase mine. Let all things that do not please God depart from my life forever, in the name of Jesus. I break and loose myself from all evil counselors. Lord, strike my enemies to fail in the day of battle. Father Lord, double my strength in the day of battle, in the name of Jesus.

Every calamity rising up against my life, I cast you down by force, in the name of Jesus. Lord, build my house and make my enemies' houses desolate. Father Lord, strengthen me in the time of trouble, in the name of Jesus.

DECREE 72

Every yoke of marital destruction in my life, break to pieces, in the name of Jesus. Every yoke of spiritual and physical bareness in my life, break. Every yoke of poverty in my life, break by fire. Every yoke of sickness and disease in my life, break, in the name of Jesus. Every yoke of untimely death in my life, break. Every yoke of memory failure in my life, break forever, in the name of Jesus. Every yoke of business failure in my life, break. Father Lord, deliver me from the yoke of demotion, in the name of Jesus. I command every yoke of witchcraft in my life to break, in the name of Jesus.

Every power scattering what I am gathering, die by fire, in the name of Jesus. I break and lose myself from the yoke of sexual immorality. Every yoke of iniquity and bad habits in my life, break, in the name of Jesus. Let the power that is in charge of my rising and falling, perish. Every seed of frustration at the edge of my breakthrough, perish, in the name of Jesus.

I command the anointing of 'almost-there' and back to square one to break, in the name of Jesus. Every problem in my life from water spirits, perish. Let witchcraft powers hovering over my life, catch fire, in the name of Jesus.

Every throne of witchcraft raised against me, be dethroned forever, in the name of Jesus. Every witchcraft load in every area of my life, I shake you off. I command the ministry of witchcraft in my life to fail. Every garment of tribulation and sorrow in my life, be roasted by fire, in the name of Jesus. Every evil flow of frustration into my life, be terminated by fire. Blood of Jesus, flush out every evil deposit in my life. Every witchcraft judgment over my life, be reversed by fire, in the name of Jesus.

Every witchcraft altar, ministering against my destiny, burn to ashes, in the name of Jesus. I break and loose myself from inherited witchcraft bondages. Every witchcraft power that has dominated every area of my life, perish, in the name of Jesus. I subdue the kingdom of witchcraft in my neighborhood, I cut off every evil soul-tie I inherited from my place of birth, in the name of Jesus. I withdraw my name from every evil register. Let every agenda of witchcraft against my destiny be frustrated, in the name of Jesus.

I receive anointing to prevail over household witchcraft, in the name of Jesus. I withdraw all my blessings from the captivity of witchcrafts. Every witch or wizard that has vowed to disgrace my life, I damage your life, in the name of Jesus. Every evil brain in the kingdom of darkness thinking about my life, receive shock and scatter. I command every spirit of witchcraft in my life to be cast out, in the name of Jesus. Every evil structure standing in my life, catch fire and burn to ashes. I withdraw my captured finances from evil covens, in the name of Jesus. Every evil that will ever take place in my dream must favor me for good. Every evil seed planted in my life while I slept, I cast you out, in the name of Jesus.

Every property of devil in my life, be roasted by fire, in the name of Jesus. Every evil covenant holding my destiny captive, break. Let every curse in my life expire. Let the earth and heavens rise up and suffocate all my problems, in the name of Jesus. Let every destructive weapon of devil against my life be shattered. Let the thunder of God tear apart every evil relationship in my life, in the name of Jesus. I frustrate evil authority of every wicked person against me. I receive complete deliverance from all night attackers in the dream, in the name of Jesus.

Every manipulation under the waters against my life, stop, in the name of Jesus. Every domineering evil power attacking my life, perish. Every power enticing me to eat in the dream, perish. Every written and unwritten agreement between me and evil powers, be broken, in the name of Jesus. Every accident devil and his agents have planned against me, backfire. Let the sacrifice of Lord Jesus terminated every evil sacrifice request over my life, in the name of Jesus. Father Lord, remove every obstacle on my way to freedom. Let the stronghold of my spirit wife or husband be pulled down, in the name of Jesus. I take back everything that belongs to me from the devil. Every spiritual battle going on against my life, be terminated to my favor, in the name of Jesus.

DECREE 73

I vomit every serpentine poison circulating all over my body, in the name of Jesus. I withdraw my private part from actors of marine kingdom. I take back my destiny from actors of the marine kingdom. Every enchantment going on against my life under the waters, stop. Every snake living inside my reproductive organ, come out and perish, in the name of Jesus. I command every dragon in charge of my case to die by force. Every program of leviathan against my life, be terminated. You my household enemies, I frustrate all your evil efforts, in the name of Jesus.

Every unclean spirit prolonging my deliverance, die in shame, in the name of Jesus. Every strange fire burning in my home, be quenched. Every sexual relationship prepared to render me useless, I reject you, in the name of Jesus. Father Lord, boil my body with Your Holy Ghost fire. Every enemy of my freedom this year, perish. Blood of Jesus, speak me out of every problem, in the name of Jesus. Hand of God, take me to my promise land. Let angels of the living God rise up and fight my battle, in the name of Jesus. Every evil personality that is assigned to rape me in my dreams, perish, in the name of Jesus. I separate my life completely from every evil power. Every defeat I have suffered last year, be converted to victory this year, in the name of Jesus.

DECREE 74

Blessed Holy Spirit, inject Your power into my system for victory. Lord, help me to stand and be rooted deeply in Your Word, in the name of Jesus. Every power that does not want me to move forward this year, perish. Lord, arise and let all my enemies scatter in shame, in the name of Jesus. Let axe of deliverance enter into my foundation now and destroy all curses. I break and lose myself from foundational bondage. Blood of Jesus, flush out every evil inheritance in my life, in the name of Jesus. Every corrupt thing deposited in my head, be cleansed. Let the creative power of God begin to function in my life, in the name of Jesus.

I reverse every evil pronouncement ever said against my life, in the name of Jesus. Every yoke of weakness and infirmity in my life, break. Let resurrection power of God enter into my life and quicken my body, in the name of Jesus. Father Lord, empower me to arise and shine forever. Every fake anointing seeking access into my life, perish. Father Lord, soak me in the stream of the source of Your power, in the name of Jesus. I command every evil remote controlling power out of my life. I break and lose myself from environmental bondages, in the name of Jesus. I stand against the strongman of my father's house to the end. Every evil assignment to waste my life, be terminated. I lift every satanic embargo placed upon my life, in the name of Jesus.

DECREE 75

Every evil bird eating the strength of my life, die by fire, in the name of Jesus. Every evil decision against my life in the spirit, scatter and fail. Every damage done to my life from evil kingdom, be repaired. I recover every good thing I ever lost to devil, in the name of Jesus. I take back thrones devil has stolen from my ancestors. I command my falling star to begin to arise and never to fall again, in the name of Jesus. Lord, arise and saturate my destiny with Your power. Let my destiny become too hot to be destroyed by devil. Every power that wants me to compromise my faith, be frustrated, in the name of Jesus.

Every evil power that has vowed to defile me this year, die in shame, in the name of Jesus. I command evil elders to start fighting themselves. Every satanic worm in my roof, die and be cast out. Every environmental chain of bondage in my life, break, in the name of Jesus. Every agent of devil controlling my destiny, be exposed and disgraced. I command all forces of darkness militating against my life to perish. Blood of Jesus, arise and better my life. Every evil tree bearing evil fruits against me, be uprooted, in the name of Jesus.

Every yoke of sleeping sickness in my life, perish, in the name of Jesus. Every power that keeps me awake when I suppose to sleep, perish. Every power preventing me from enjoying my sleep, die by force, in the name of Jesus.

DECREE 76

Every problem that has root in my life, be uprooted by blood of Jesus, in the name of Jesus. Every good door closed against my life, open by force. Every area of my life that is barren of every good thing, be delivered. Every arrow of demonic frustration fired against my life, I fire you back, in the name of Jesus. I command every bondage in my life to be broken by force. Let all my efforts to succeed in life be successful by fire, in the name of Jesus. Let every arrow of disaster fired against my life backfire. I command every area of my life experiencing ups and downs to be set free, in the name of Jesus.

I fire back every arrow of lusts and uncontrollable desires for immorality. I break and lose myself from the anointing of the tail, in the name of Jesus. Every tortoise and snail anointing in my life, break. Let the fire of God burn to ashes every cobweb in my life, in the name of Jesus. Lord, empower me to understand people and to be able to relate well. I disgrace every evil power exposing me to satanic attacks. I command all evil forces assigned to close down my businesses to die today. Every mysterious evil action about to take place in my life, receive death, in the name of Jesus.

I refuse to lose every money to devil, in the name of Jesus. Lord, empower me to keep my job, money and wealth to your glory, in the name of Jesus. Every pain in Every part of my body, whether you like it or not, stop, in the name of Jesus. Every evil desire in my life, perish. Lord, arise and promote every good thing in my life, in the name of Jesus.

DECREE 77

I renounce every evil connection and dedication to the marine kingdom, in the name of Jesus. I close up every evil mouth speaking against my destiny. Every power crying against my deliverance, be frustrated. Every persistent problem in my life, your time is up, perish. Every demon against my deliverance, I cast you out, in the name of Jesus. Every enemy of God's level of righteousness in my life, perish. Every enemy of divine health in my life, I cut off your head, in the name of Jesus.

Every spiritual armed robber tormenting my life, be tormented to death, in the name of Jesus. Let heaven and earth begin to frustrate my entire unrepentant enemies. Every domineering power of darkness against my life, be weakened, in the name of Jesus. Every document written against my life, be roasted by fire. Every evil activity going on against my life, be terminated, in the name of Jesus. Father Lord, bring Your true deliverance into my life. Let all my evil relatives be frustrated until they repent, in the name of Jesus.

I command my reproductive organ to escape every satanic judgment, in the name of Jesus. Every strongman hindering my marital progress, die in shame. Let the thunder of God tear apart every enemy of my prosperity. Every scorpion of darkness oppressing my destiny, perish, in the name of Jesus. Every wicked personality vomiting strange fire into my life, die by your fire. Holy Ghost fire, charge my blood against every sickness, in the name of Jesus.

DECREE 78

Every evil actor commanding strange fire into my life, be destroyed, in the name of Jesus. Every agent of confusion on assignment against my life, be frustrated. Every instrument of destruction fashioned against my destiny, perish, in the name of Jesus. I command every satanic satellite monitoring my life to be blinded. Every evil work going on against my life, I stop you by force, in the name of Jesus. I command every grave that has swallowed my blessings to vomit them by force. Every evil hand planting rubbish into my life, wither, in the name of Jesus.

Every part of my life enemies has converted into rags, be delivered by fire, in the name of Jesus. Blood of Jesus, speak deliverance into every area of my life. Every power blocking my vision, clear away, in the name of Jesus. Lord, release Your favor into my life. Every evil rain prepared against my life this year; I avoid you. Father Lord, take me away from evil captivities, in the name of Jesus. I receive power of self-control this year. Lord, help me to be faithful to Your Word forever, in the name of Jesus.

Father Lord, increase my helpers this year to Your own glory, in the name of Jesus. Every death devil has planned for my family, fail woefully. I receive grace to walk in integrity forever, in the name of Jesus. Father Lord, arise and help me to fulfill my dreams in life. Every enemy of God's plan for my life, be exposed and disgraced, in the name of Jesus.

DECREE 79

I bring the oil of the Holy Ghost upon every rusted nut in my life, in the name of Jesus. Let peace of God suppress every chaos organized against my life. Every evil power taking upper hand in my life, perish, in the name of Jesus. I terminate every evil agreement between men and my enemies. Every evil consultation against my life, be frustrated, in the name of Jesus. Lord, arise and contend with my contenders. Every reporting demon following me about, be frustrated. I receive divine immunity against demonic attacks this year, in the name of Jesus.

I bring blood of Jesus against satanic barriers on my way this year, in the name of Jesus. Every witchcraft meeting organized against my life, scatter. Father Lord, arise and organize my life for the best, in the name of Jesus. Lord Jesus, upgrade my brain by fire, in the name of Jesus. I retrieve all my lost blessings from the kingdom of darkness. Every satanic calendar against my life, be dismantled, in the name of Jesus. Every satanic priest ministering against my life, receive destruction. I pull down every negative plan concluded against my life, in the name of Jesus.

Father Lord, empower me to possess the gates of my enemies, in the name of Jesus. Lord Jesus, anoint me with the oil of gladness. Every satanic checkpoint standing against my life, be dismantled, in the name of Jesus. Every satanic television mounted against me, break. I puncture every evil eye monitoring my destiny, in the name of Jesus.

DECREE 80

Every power that has vowed to waste my finance this year, perish, in the name of Jesus. Blood of Jesus, flow into my foundation and begin to cleanse me. Holy Ghost fire, burn to ashes every enemy of my breakthrough. Everlasting God, give me everlasting miracles this year, in the name of Jesus. Every enemy of my rest, you are wicked, perish. I throw off every burden of poverty and disgrace in my life, in the name of Jesus. Every power that wants to entangle my life with problems, perish. Every evil movement against my blessings, I stop you now, in the name of Jesus.

Every evil counsel against my destiny this year, be rejected completely, in the name of Jesus. Every evil messenger assigned to me this year, take your message to your sender. Every hidden problem in my life, be exposed to death. I command every altar of darkness militating against me to be destroyed. Blood of Jesus, flow into Every evil river working against my destiny, in the name of Jesus. Every marine spirit shrine ministering against my life, be roasted by fire. Father Lord, give me a testimony that will shake the world, in the name of Jesus.

Every satanic roadblock mounted up against my life, be dismantled, in the name of Jesus. I release terrible fear into the apartment of my enemies. Lord, arise and unburden my life from evil burdens, in the name of Jesus. Every satanic attack planned against my life this year, backfire. Father Lord, give me explosive miracles of 'how-did-it-happen' this year, in the name of Jesus. Let the wind of destruction destroy my enemies' strongholds this year. Every serpent in every dark place of my life, come out and perish, in the name of Jesus.

Let the anger of God explode in the camp of my enemies this year, in the name of Jesus. Father Lord, help me to trample upon serpents and scorpions this year. Every arrow of death fired against me this year, backfire, in the name of Jesus. Father Lord, use this year to meet me at the point of all my needs. Every enemy of my joy shall become sorrowful from henceforth. Every power that wants me to die without bring fulfilled, perish, in the name of Jesus. All satanic music playing against me this year, I reject you, in the name of Jesus.

Every evil attached to my name, I cast you out by force, in the name of Jesus. I receive divine grace to match upon the heads of my enemies. Every problem designed to finish me up this year, die before your time. Every evil personality that is hired to set me up, perish, in the name of Jesus. Lord, disgrace my stubborn enemies this year. Lord, arise and change my situation, in the name of Jesus. Every bread of sorrow prepared for me this year, be eaten by my enemies. Every power challenging God in my life, be disgraced, in the name of Jesus. Every satanic limitation in my destiny, disappear. Every dream of failure designed against my life, perish, in the name of Jesus.

DECREE 81

Father Lord, cause Your goodness to reach my life this year, in the name of Jesus. Let the wonderful work of God promote my destiny this year. I command every imperfection in my life this year to be perfected, in the name of Jesus. Every power that wants to take the place of God in my life, perish. Every power abusing God in my life, die without mercy, in the name of Jesus. Every disgrace fashioned against my life this year, backfire. I reject every package of defeat with my name this year. I convert all my disappointments into divine appointments in this year, in the name of Jesus.

Every evil wind directed against my life, locate your sender, in the name of Jesus. Every evil worm eating up my life, die without delay. Every witch or wizard that has swallowed my miracle, vomit it now, in the name of Jesus. Every enemy of my greatness, be wasted. Father Lord, bring Your everlasting joy and peace into my life, in the name of Jesus. Every spirit of poverty disgracing me everywhere, be disgraced. I reject the position that devil has given to me in life. Lord, help me to walk into Your plan for my life, in the name of Jesus. Every enemy of my destiny, perish. I shall arise and prosper beyond others in my area of specialization, in the name of Jesus.

I recover all my wasted years in sin. Every embarrassment prepared against me this year, I reject you, in the name of Jesus. Lord, arise and embarrass me with miracles. Every evil seed abort to germinate in my life, perish, in the name of Jesus. I destroy every demon against my miracle this year. Lord, arise and fix me up in life, in the name of Jesus. Every womb that has swallowed my finances, open and release them. I receive the anointing to prosper beyond my imagination, in the name of Jesus. I command my lost glory to come back double by fire. Father Lord, give me great open doors this year by fire, in the name of Jesus.

Every enemy of my breakthrough mocking my life, perish, in the name of Jesus. Every word the enemy has spoken against my destiny, perish. Every evil judgment passed against my life, be reversed by force, in the name of Jesus. I command the wind of God to carry away every problem in my life. I command my enemies to perish at my presence, in the name of Jesus. Every evil movement against my life, backfire immediately. I refuse to cooperate or agree with devil and his agents in evil. Every evil personality that has vowed to attack me, attack yourself and perish, in the name of Jesus. to devil, I recover you double.

Let my enemies make mistakes that will favor me this year and forever, in the name of Jesus. Let every mischief planned against my life be fulfilled on the heads of my enemies, in the name of Jesus. Every instrument of death prepared against my life, kill your owner. I run away from the place my enemy has planned to waste my life, in the name of Jesus. Father Lord, frustrate all my problems in life, in the name of Jesus.

Lord, refuse to grant devil and his agents their heart desires over my life, in the name of Jesus. Let shame visit my enemies whatever they are this year. I command every problem in my life to be taken away far from me. I command my ways this year to be mightily blessed, in the name of Jesus. Father Lord, prepare me for miraculous explosions this year, in the name of Jesus.

Every evil counsel against my life, be converted to foolishness, in the name of Jesus. Every evil displacement of my destiny in every place against my life, be reversed. Every enemy of my soul this year, be exposed and be disgraced, in the name of Jesus. Blood of Jesus, speak my life out of every trouble this year, in Jesus name. Father Lord, reverse every evil action against me this year. Blood of Jesus, swallow my problems this year, in the name of Jesus. Every weapon of frustration against my life, become blunt. Let my enemies be dashed to pieces like potter's vessel. Let the sword of fire cut my unrepentant enemies to pieces, in the name of Jesus.

Every satanic embargo against my businesses, be lifted, in the name of Jesus. Let strange flies in my life receive fire and death. Every judgment against my handwork, be reversed, in the name of Jesus. Lord, develop every undeveloped area of my life this year. Blood of Jesus, empower my tongue to speak out your greatness, in the name of Jesus. I release all my organs detained by Satan. Father Lord, anoint me to face every challenge this year unto victory. Every spell, curses and enchantment against my life, be cancelled. Blood of Jesus, remove my confusion forever. I command the eagle of my life to mount up with wings to the top, in the name of Jesus.

Every power assigned to bring me down to the ground, perish, in the name of Jesus. Let my rising this year be made continuous by the power of God. Let the joy of the Almighty God sustain me with divine strength this year, in the name of Jesus. I receive power to be the reference point for good this year. I lose myself from the bondage in my place of birth, in the name of Jesus. Let God's fire consume every evil sacrifice offered against my life. I command angels of the Lord to execute judgment against my stubborn enemies this year, in the name of Jesus.

Every satanic blockage to my breakthrough, be removed this year. Every satanic success in my life, be destroyed, in the name of Jesus. Father Lord, cause me to swim in the sea of prosperity forever, in the name of Jesus. Let every branch of my life receive divine touch. I block every evil power from entering into my life this year, in the name of Jesus. Let divine move bring me to a place of prosperity this year. Holy Ghost fire, deliver me today, in the name of Jesus.

DECREE 82

Blood of Jesus cancel every known and unknown curse in my life, in the name of Jesus. I command every ancestral demon to move out of my way forever. Every evil river flowing into my life, dry up by fire, in the name of Jesus. Every influence of household enemy in my life, be destroyed. Every satanic investment in my life, be wasted, in the name of Jesus. I soak my life in blood of Jesus for signs and wonders. I disallow every enemy of my greatness to enter into my life, in the name of Jesus. Let satanic agents assigned to confuse me perish. I receive deliverance from altars of my place of birth, in the name of Jesus.

I cover my brain and every organ of my life with the blood of Jesus, in the name of Jesus. Every evil foundation raised everywhere against my life; I pull you down. Every problem linking me with death, destroy yourself and perish, in the name of Jesus. Every water in my environment announcing my death, be troubled to death. Let every enemy of my glory be demoted by force. Lord, help me to become Your battle axe in this generation, in the name of Jesus. Every power that has vowed to useless my life, be useless. Let the wisdom of my enemies be converted to foolishness, in the name of Jesus.

Every power standing in the gate of my life to fool me, be cast out, in the name of Jesus. I resign every position I hold in the kingdom of darkness unconsciously. Lord, select me and bless me this year, in the name of Jesus. Every book that devil has written about me, be consumed by fire. I break and lose myself from evil controls, in the name of Jesus. Let the blood of Jesus be transfused into my blood. Every evil gate blocking my way to my rights, be opened by force. I command every foundational strongman against my life to collapse and perish, in the name of Jesus.

I break and lose myself from consequences of my ancestral sins, in the name of Jesus. I command every problem that has entered into my life through sexual sin to perish. I deliver myself from evil foods I ate in the dream, in the name of Jesus. Let the chain of evil association in my life break by force. I dismantle every satanic hindrance to my progress this year. Let the east wind blow away every evil power on my way, in the name of Jesus. Every wicked personality that has vowed to stand against my life, perish, in the name of Jesus.

Let every force militating against my life die this year, in the name of Jesus. Let all the wickedness of evil people against my life backfire. Lord, disorganize every evil coalition power against my life, in the name of Jesus. Every bitter water in my life, dry up. Every fire of confusion burning in my life, be quenched by force, in the name of Jesus. I receive back every good thing that enemies have stolen from my life. Every evil vehicle moving away my blessings, bring them back by force, in the name of Jesus. I fire back every evil arrow fired at my life, Lord, save me from every problem, in the name of Jesus.

Every foolish demon delaying my deliverance, drink death and perish, in the name of Jesus. Every wise fool in the battlefield of my life, be wasted by death. Every good thing devil has stolen from my life, I recover you now, in the name of Jesus. Let God arise and trouble my troubles. Every satanic chain holding me down in one spot, break to pieces, in the name of Jesus. Father Lord, make a way for me and take me to a place of safety. Every satanic giant in my promise land, die and die forever, in the name of Jesus.

Blood of Jesus, flow into my Red Sea and dry it for my sake, in the name of Jesus. Every Goliath in the battlefield to waste my destiny, be wasted. Every evil deed done against my life at night, be converted to my favor, in the name of Jesus. Every man, woman or power that has vowed to kill me this year, kill yourself. Every problem manipulating my life, be manipulated to death, in the name of Jesus.

I command every problem in my life to disappear and let my glory appear, in the name of Jesus. Every evil voice campaigning to rearrange my life, be silenced by divine fire. Lord, deliver me from every problem you allowed into my life, in the name of Jesus. Every power causing me to operate below standards, perish. I destroy every information devil is using to torment my life. Every satanic power attacking my destiny, become impotent. Every evil power polluting my life, be paralyzed by fire, in the name of Jesus. Every evil done against my life from the womb, be corrected. Fire of God, burn to ashes every problem in my life, in the name of Jesus.

I restore my life from evil altars. Let the earth vomit all my blessings buried in it by force, in the name of Jesus. Every power in charge of denoting my life, be frustrated. Every evil lender presiding over my life, be dethroned by force, in the name of Jesus. Let the powers of darkness in charge of darkness over my life perish. Every power eating my glory, be wasted by fire, in the name of Jesus. Every evil transaction done against my life, be nullified. Every manipulation taking place against my life, stop by force, in the name of Jesus. Every evil spirit attacking me because of my name, perish. Every rag of poverty in my life, be roasted by fire, in the name of Jesus.

Every witch or wizard that has swallowed my original self, vomit it, in the name of Jesus. Let my excellence rise above others by fire. Let all arrested demons in my life, be executed now, in the name of Jesus. Angels of the living God, arise, open evil prisons and release me. Let enemies of my freedom enter into bondage for my sake, in the name of Jesus. Every power withholding what will make me great this year, release then to me. Every dark agent contending with my blessings, be destroyed. Let all my stolen greatness be recovered by force, in the name of Jesus. Father Lord, take me from where I am now to where I am supposed to be. Every bad leg that has walked into my apartment, walk out now by fire, in the name of Jesus.

DECREE 83

Every agent of devil jubilating over my life, begin to mourn, in the name of Jesus. Every blessing I have lost to water spirits, I recover you double. Let the rivers of the living water flow into my life, in the name of Jesus. I command every wicked bird that is flying because of me to perish. Every power that has exchange my glory, return it back by force, in the name of Jesus. Father Lord, send the Prince of peace to bring peace into my life. Let the benefit of Messiah's reign begin to manifest in my life. Every war going on against my life, cease by force forever. Every evil kingdom standing against my progress, scatter, in the name of Jesus.

Let my life come under the design of Christ this year and forever, in the name of Jesus. I command economic prosperity from Christ to manifest in my life. Blood of Jesus, increase my joy to overflow this year, in the name of Jesus. I bring myself under the perfect leadership of the King of kings. Lord, send Your comforter to comfort me greatly this year. Lord Jesus, arise and minister to me in every area of my life, in the name of Jesus. I receive justice this year for all injustices I have suffered in the past. Let the knowledge of Christ introduce me to other knowledge that I need, in the name of Jesus.

Every curse that refused to let me go, be removed by Christ, in the name of Jesus. I receive the grace that will give me abundant productivity this year. Every evil venom in my life, be removed by force. I command the strength of every sickness in my life to be removed, in the name of Jesus. I destroy every destroyer of my health this year. Lord Jesus, correct every deformity in my life this year, in the name of Jesus. Let my life be preserved in health till I fulfill my destiny. I receive freedom from every oppressor this year, in the name of Jesus.

Anointing to enter into a life of fellowship with God, possess me this year, in the name of Jesus. Father Lord, lead me to a life of rest all the days of my life. Every enemy of righteousness of God in my life, be wasted, in the name of Jesus. I obtain favor from God to enter into life of His service this year. Blood of Jesus, bring Your glory fully back into my life this year, in the name of Jesus. Power to hunger no more and be sick no more, possess me. Lord Jesus, open my mouth and feed me with heavenly food, in the name of Jesus. Let the tree of life in heaven command healing into my life. Every source of pain in my life, perish, in the name of Jesus. Power to live a transparent life from this year, possess me, in the name of Jesus. Every divine door closed against my life, open this year. Every evil obstruction blocking my way to heavenly blessings, be removed, in the name of Jesus. Let the mark of God for my successes begin to manifest. Lord, arise and bring blessings into my life this year. Every satanic plan against my life, be exposed and disgraced this year, in the name of Jesus.

DECREE 84

Let God arise and frustrate enemies of my righteousness this year, in the name of Jesus. Every demon diverting progresses out my life, receive confusion. I reject every satanic appointment opened up for me this year, in the name of Jesus. Every incantation designed to destroy my life this year, fail woefully. Every witchcraft ritual directed against my destiny, expire, in the name of Jesus. I render null and void every evil influence against my breakthrough this year. Let my household enemies drink confusion by fire, in the name of Jesus.

Let the forces of darkness working against my future be scattered, in the name of Jesus. Let the rod of the wicked designed to rest upon me be removed. Every evil spirit I have invited into my life, I cast you out, in the name of Jesus. Father Lord, command Your light to shine into my life. Every stubborn curse militating against my destiny, fail woefully. Every power that has vowed to divert my glory, be frustrated, in the name of Jesus. Lord, help me to fulfil my destiny. All my blessings stolen in the dream, be recovered double. Every arrow of vanity fired into my life, come out and go back to your sender, in the name of Jesus.

Every evil mouth opened to swallow my glory, close, in the name of Jesus. Blood of Jesus flow into my life and correct every error. Every forest demon attacking my life, I cast you out, in the name of Jesus. Every demon attacking me from the rocks, perish. Every evil hand pulling me backward, dry up, in the name of Jesus. Father Lord, help me to move forward to Your own place of blessings. I recover myself from every great loss in the past. Every local charm delaying my progress, be roasted by fire, in the name of Jesus. Every evil sacrifice keeping me under evil control, explode by fire. I break and loose myself from marine spirit bondage, in the name of Jesus.

God of signs and wonders, do Your signs and wonders in my life, in the name of Jesus. Every satanic vulture assigned against my life, perish. Every evil chain dragging my destiny up and down, break, in the name of Jesus. Lord, arise and starve my problems to death. Every family idol holding me in bondage, catch fire, in the name of Jesus. Every satanic agent controlling my progress, be frustrated. Every power from the waters dominating my life, be dominated, in the name of Jesus. Every government of suffering in my life, be roasted by fire. Every evil veil covering my glory, be roasted by fire. Lord, deliver me from living a false life, in the name of Jesus. I break and loose myself from every deeply entrenched problem. Arrows of day and night fired at my life, locate your sender, in the name of Jesus.

Every satanic thief assigned to my life, be exposed to death, in the name of Jesus. Every evil plantation in my life, perish. Arrows of strange fire fired against my life, backfire, in the name of Jesus. I use the blood of Jesus against every problem in my life this year. Every power of darkness prolonging my bondage, perish, in the name of Jesus. Every area of my destiny captured by devil, be released. Every strongman that has hijacked my life, release it by force. Let the backbone of my destiny destroyers break to pieces, in the name of Jesus. Every satanic spy monitoring my life, be blinded to death. Every evil power that has swallowed my money, vomit it now, in the name of Jesus.

Every serpent of darkness manipulating my brain, die by fire, in the name of Jesus. Every power commissioned to arrest my progress this year, perish. Every satanic minister ministering evil into my life, perish, in the name of Jesus. Agent of devil promoting poverty in my life, be wasted. Every coffin spirit that has buried my destiny, release it now, in the name of Jesus. Spirit of the graveyard attacking my life, go back to the grave and perish, in the name of Jesus. I deliver my life from spirit of shame and disgrace. Blood of Jesus, deliver me from 'roundabout' spirits. Every vagabond spirit that refused to let me go, die by fire, in the name of Jesus.

I command spirits in the rocks or altars to release my greatness, in the name of Jesus. Every evil power attacking my life from the forest, go back to your place. I reject every counterfeit spirit, in the name of Jesus. Father Lord, deliver me from shame. Lord, arise and fight my battles. I break and loose myself from death and hell, in the name of Jesus. I separate myself from evil observers, in the name of Jesus.

I break and loose myself from satanic revivals. Every strange money inside my money, I remove you now, in the name of Jesus. Father Lord, destroy Every evil plan of the wicked against my life. I command every evil bullet in my life to come out by fire. Blood of Jesus hide me from attacks of desert spirits, in the name of Jesus. I move out from every satanic field of destruction. I command every spirit of tragedy to loose hold over my life. Every power assigned to amputate my breakthrough, be destroyed, in the name of Jesus. Every visible or invisible mark of devil in my life, disappear. Every wicked witch or wizard against my progress in life, die by fire, in the name of Jesus.

Every evil mouth reporting me to evil kingdom, close forever, in the name of Jesus. Let all satanic broadcasting equipment's against me burn to ashes. I command every dark agent working against my life to perish. Every evil angel that has vowed to waste my life, be wasted, in the name of Jesus. I break and lose myself from every concrete curse. I command all multiple gains of Satan in my life to flop, in the name of Jesus. Every power that has bewitched my handiwork, be destroyed. Let every marriage-killing spirit be arrested for my marriage's sake, in the name of Jesus.

DECREE 85

Every evil plantation in the foundation of my life, perish, in the name of Jesus. Blood of Jesus, destroy my personal stronghold this year for Your glory. Every gate of the wicked in my life, be removed by force, in the name of Jesus. Every power transferring my blessings to satanic banks, fall down and perish. Every satanic opinion about my life, be rejected, in the name of Jesus. Evil wasters of great destined people, l am not your candidate, fall away. Every satanic reinforcement against my life, be disgraced, in the name of Jesus.

You my pocked with holes, be mended by fire, in the name of Jesus. Every power that has caged my finance, release it now. Let my personal territorial demotion receive divine promotion, in the name of Jesus. I expose and destroy all my hidden oppressors. Every agent of devil hindering my angel of blessing, perish, in the name of Jesus. Every satanic prayer going on against my life, backfire. I refuse to attend to shame distributor in my life, in the name of Jesus.

I cast out of my life the spirit of late progress, in the name of Jesus. Owners of evil loads in my life, appear and carry your loads to the grave. Every evil deposit in my life, perish, in the name of Jesus. I fire back every occultic arrow fired at my life. Every satanic property in my life, perish. Blood of Jesus, speak death to every false prophesy against me, in the name of Jesus. Every satanic bank that has seized my finance, release it now. Let the destroying flood of God destroy my destroyers. Let the bones of my unrepentant enemies break to pieces, in the name of Jesus.

Let the earth of my stubborn enemies' quake by force, in the name of Jesus. Every agent of Satan attacking me from the waters, be disgraced. Let brimstone of judgment pursued all my pursuers, in the name of Jesus. You my unrepentant enemy, open your mouth and eat bread of afflictions. Every oppressor of my destiny, receive bitter destruction, in the name of Jesus. Every problem raging against my life, be destroyed. Let the world rise up against all my problems now, in the name of Jesus. Every power that refused to cooperate with God in my life, perish. You my spiritual evil parent, I disown you now, in the name of Jesus.

You unprofitable ventures designed to destroy me, I reject you, in the name of Jesus. I shake evil foundations built against my destiny. Every evil symbol standing against my life, be pulled down, in the name of Jesus. Every good thing I need in my life, begin to come now. Holy Ghost fire, burn every enemy of my peace, in the name of Jesus. Let my God arise and defend me. Father Lord, pull me out from Every strange relationship, in the name of Jesus.

DECREE 86

I command every satanic investment in my life to perish, in the name of Jesus. Every evil program against my life, perish. Let evil pronouncement against my blessings be wasted, in the name of Jesus. Every evil arrest against my position, be released. Every good thing I have lost to devil. I recover you completely, in the name of Jesus.

Every spiritual warfare going on against my life, end to my favor. I speak death against all my problems, in the name of Jesus. I destroy every demonic dominion over my life. I command evil powers sitting upon my blessings to perish. I speak death unto every evil voice raised against me, in the name of Jesus.

I pull down every problem that has exalted itself over me, in the name of Jesus. I speak from the heavens against every evil authority in my territory. Every evil power reigning over my life, be dethroned. Blood of Jesus, pour upon the heads of my enemies, in the name of Jesus. I cut off the head of strongman of my father's house. I speak death to every problem programmed into the sun against me, in the name of Jesus. You the sun, reverse every curse programmed into you against me, in the name of Jesus.

DECREE 87

I release destruction from the sun against my stubborn enemies, in the name of Jesus. Let the sun hunt to death every destroyer of my life. You the sun, refuse to honor every evil word against my life this year, in the name of Jesus. Wherever my enemies are coming from, let sun smite them. You the sun, revolt against every incantation made against my life, in the name of Jesus. I command the moon to pursue my enemies to destruction. Every evil thing programmed into the moon against my life, perish, in the name of Jesus.

Lord, arise and use the moon to defend my life, in the name of Jesus. Blood of Jesus, arise and silence my problems. Let fire arise from the sun to defend me, in the name of Jesus. Every evil personality working to arrest my life, I arrest your star. Let fire of God burn to ashes the stars behind my problems. Every enemy of my life, be frustrated to death, in the name of Jesus. Let every wicked star against my life this year by locked up by God, I arrest to death the stars of my occultic enemies, in the name of Jesus.

Let waters of death fill the mouths of the wicked, in the name of Jesus. Every enemy of my destiny, be troubled by the waters in your belly. I command the waters all over the world to fight my enemies, in the name of Jesus. Let the waters on earth and the heavenlies trouble my troubles. I command fire to move around now and burn my problems to ashes. Wherever my enemies are hiding. Let the Holy Ghost fire locate and burn them. Fire of God, move forward and deliver me, in the name of Jesus.

I command penetrating power of God to use fire against all my failures, in the name of Jesus. I command fire to purge my body of every problem. Let the fire of God shine into dark areas of my life, in the name of Jesus.

DECREE 88

Blood of Jesus and fire of God, deliver me this year, in the name of Jesus. Let shining and enlightening power of God expose my problems to death. Let the air move towards my enemies' camps and waste them. Every evil air directed against my life, backfire. I enter into the air to waste my destiny wasters. Let the air of destruction enter into the camp of my enemies. Every satanic road block against my life, be removed by air, in the name of Jesus. Every evil power monitoring my life, I destroy you by air. I destroy my problems everywhere they exist and command them to vanish, in the name of Jesus.

Every evil movement against my life, be arrested by air, in the name of Jesus. Let the air carry message of death to all wicked personalities against me. I release messengers of death by air into every witchcraft gathering, in the name of Jesus. I command the air to scatter all my unrepentant enemies. Let destructive tempest enter into the waters and fight for me. I walk into the cloud to put an end to every evil work against me. Let thunder from the third heavens blow off my enemies, in the name of Jesus.

I release angry lightening to kill every problem in my life, in the name of Jesus. Let hail stones from God fall upon the heads of my stubborn enemies. Angels of God, release hailstones into the camp of my enemies. Let destructive rain fall from heaven upon wicked persons against my life, in the name of Jesus. I command rain of death to enter the camp of the wicked. Let rain of destruction visit the sun, moon and waters for my sake, in the name of Jesus. Blood of Jesus, speak death to idols of my father's house. Let the snow of death overshadow my stubborn enemies. Let my sickness die by the dew of heaven, in the name of Jesus.

DECREE 89

Whoever makes use of water to fight against me shall die by water, in the name of Jesus. Let waters of God on earth rise against all my enemies. I convert waters that my enemies use to rise against them, in the name of Jesus. Let waters flow in abundance and destroy the camps of my enemies. Let my enemies be oppressed by waters wherever water exists, in the name of Jesus. Let the depth of the waters swallow up my enemies and problems. I command destructive powers in the waters to destroy my enemies. Let my enemies perish before waters, in the name of Jesus.

You the earth, open up and swallow my problems, in the name of Jesus. You the earth, refuse to honor every evil sacrifice done against me. Let every evil my enemies raised against my life be buried in the dust. Every power behind my problems, be buried in the earth. I command the morning to swallow my problems, in the name of Jesus. I command the night to kill all my problems I command the atmosphere to kill every evil raised against me. Let all the elements join forces to destroy my enemies, in the name of Jesus.

DECREE 90

I raise Holy Ghost altar against the wicked, in the name of Jesus. I raise divine altars among the entire creations to destroy my destroyers. I command every creature to rise up and fight for me. Let bedroom, sitting room, car, office and all places on earth where evil is planned against me fight for me. I use weapons of my enemies against them, in the name of Jesus. Let everything my enemies have turn against them for my sake. I command every environment in all creation to favor me. Let the creatures refuse to walk against me, in the name of Jesus.

I command angels of God to fight from heavens for my sake, in the name of Jesus. I bring judgment against curses in my life. Let the entire creation convert every curse against me into blessings, in the name of Jesus. Every star representing my problems, catch fire and burn to ashes. I bring down every evil star against me in the heavenlies, in the name of Jesus. Every power behind my problems, be arrested. Let the entire creation destroy every physical and spiritual organization against my life. Let whirlwind from heaven blow off heads of the wicked. I command my personal evil stronghold to be consumed by fire, in the name of Jesus.

DECREE 91

Let great earthquake locate the camp of my enemies now, in the name of Jesus. I release seaquake to waste all my destiny wasters in the waters. I command the air to quake for my sake and destroy works of evil principalities against my life, in the name of Jesus. Horrible tempest, fall upon the camp of my enemies. Let the furnace of affliction oppress my oppressors to death, I send brimstone and fire from heavens against my unrepentant enemies, in the name of Jesus. I command madness to enter into brains of my unrepentant enemies. Fire of blindness, possess the eyes of my wicked enemies, in the name of Jesus.

Let the bones of my enemies lose their strength, in the name of Jesus. I feed all my oppressors with bread and water of affliction. I command the cloud of sorrow to cover all my enemies, in the name of Jesus. Let the unbearable heat from hell fire, burn my enemies. Let destroying flood from above sweep away my enemies. Let shock, stroke and destruction visit the wicked for my sake, in the name of Jesus. Let the wind of God take disappointments to my enemies. Let arrows of failure be relayed to my enemies, in the name of Jesus.

I command evil worms to eat up all my stubborn enemies, in the name of Jesus. Let all my problems face bitter destruction this year. I send arrows of bitter destruction to all my enemies this year, in the name of Jesus. Let all my stubborn enemies gather themselves to destruction. Whatever devil has done against my life, receive death, in the name of Jesus. Let all that agents of devil did against me die forever. Every power that will work to renew my bondage this year shall fail and perish. I raise uncompromising wrath of God against my enemies from today, in the name of Jesus.

Let the earth, sun, moon and stars, refuse to answer devil and his agents for my sake, in the name of Jesus. I instruct all the elements to fight back all my enemies from today. Every evil word that will be uttered against me from today will backfire, in the name of Jesus. Let the cloud, tempest, thunder, lightning, hailstone, rain, snow and the dew frustrate my enemies in the future. Let the entire creation begin to oppress my past, present and future enemies to death. I seal my prayers of authority with the seal of God forever, in the name of Jesus.

THANK YOU!

I'd like to use this time to thank you for purchasing my books and helping my ministry and work. Any copy of my book you buy helps to fund my ministry and family, as well as offering much-needed inspiration to keep writing. My family and I are very thankful, and we take your assistance very seriously.

You have already accomplished so much, but I would appreciate an honest review of some of my books through the link below. This is critical since reviews reflect how much an author's work is respected.

Please [click here] to leave a review on Amazon. If you're viewing from a printed version, please visit amazon.com/review/create-review?asin=B08NSB8CMS to leave a review.

Please be aware that I read and value all comments and reviews. You can always post a review even though you haven't finished the book yet, and then edit your reviews later.

Thank you so much as you spare a precious moment of your time and may God bless you and meet you at the very point of your need.

You can also send me an email to hello@madueke.com if you encounter any difficulty while writing your review.

PRAYER M. MADUEKE'S BESTSELLING BOOKS

Click on any of the [Buy Now] buttons to view or purchase them on my website. If you're viewing from a printed version, please visit madueke.com and search for these books.

1. Dictionary of Demons & Complete Deliverance [Buy Now]

2. Monitoring Spirits [Buy Now]

3. Praying with The Blood of Jesus [Buy Now]

4. The Power of Speaking in Tongues [Buy Now]

5. Speaking Things into Existence by Faith [Buy Now]

6. Discerning and Defeating the Ahab & Jezebel Spirit [Buy Now]

7. Defeating the Python Spirit [Buy Now]

8. 35 Special Dangerous Decrees [Buy Now]

9. 21/40 Nights of Decrees and Your Enemies Will Surrender [Buy Now]

10. Command the Morning, Day and Night [Buy Now]

11. Evil Summon [Buy Now]

12. Overcoming & Destroying the Spirit of Rejection & Hatred [Buy Now]

13. Queen of Heaven: Wife of Satan [Buy Now]

14. The False Prophet [Buy Now]

15. Dominion Over Sickness & Disease [Buy Now]

16. The Battle Plan for Destroying Foundational Witchcraft [Buy Now]

17. The Queen of the Coast [Buy Now]

18. Dictionary of Unmerited Favor [Buy Now]

19. Prayers for Breakthrough in your Business [Buy Now]

20. A Jump From Evil Altar [Buy Now]

21. 100 Days Prayers to Wake Up Your Lazarus [Buy Now]

22. Breaking Evil Yokes [Buy Now]

23. When Evil Altars are Multiplied [Buy Now]

24. The Battle Plan for Destroying Foundational Occultism [Buy Now]

25. Prayers for Protection   [**Buy Now**]

26. Prayers for Academic Success   [**Buy Now**]

27. Your Dream Directory   [**Buy Now**]

28. Prayers for Financial Breakthrough   [**Buy Now**]

29. Destiny and Star Hunters   [**Buy Now**]

30. Prayers to Pray during Courtship   [**Buy Now**]

31. 91 Days Decrees to Takeover the Year   [**Buy Now**]

32. Alone with God   [**Buy Now**]

33. Prayers against Satanic Oppression   [**Buy Now**]

34. Foundations Exposed   [**Buy Now**]

35. Prayers for Deliverance   [**Buy Now**]

36. Prayers to Heal Broken Relationship   [**Buy Now**]

37. Prayers for Good Health   [**Buy Now**]

38. Comprehensive Deliverance   [**Buy Now**]

39. Prayers for College and University Students   [**Buy Now**]

40. 40 Prayer Giants [**Buy Now**]

41. Divine Protection & Immunity While Sleeping [**Buy Now**]

42. Prayers for Fertility in your Marriage [**Buy Now**]

43. More Kingdoms to Conquer [**Buy Now**]

44. Confront and Conquer your Enemy [**Buy Now**]

45. Prayers to Raise Godly Children [**Buy Now**]

4 Free Ebooks

In order to say a 'Thank You' for purchasing *91 Days Decrees to Takeover the Year*, I offer these books to you in appreciation. Click or type **madueke.com/free-gift** in your browser.

Video Bonus

I've created exclusive video content to complement the topics covered in the book. These videos provide deeper insights and discussions on the things discussed in this book, offering you a more immersive learning experience.

To access the video bonus for this course, simply click or type links.madueke.com/2DTY in your browser.

Message from the Author

I want to see you succeed, grow, and break free from negativity and obstacles. My hope is for you to thrive, unaffected by negative influences and challenging situations. Because of that, please permit me to introduce two courses that I believe passionately will help you:

1. To break the evil altars and powers of your father's house, The role of altars in the realm of existence is very key because altars are meeting places between the physical and the spiritual, between the visible and the invisible.

    Unless a man cuts off the evil flow from the power of his father's house, he will not fulfil his destiny. Click here to learn more about my course on how to tear down unholy altars and close the enemy's entryways into your life!

2. To help you seamlessly break iron-like problems, illness, delayed marriage, poverty, or any long-standing battle.

    Discover the transformative power of Christian fasting and prayer. Remember, Matthew 17:21 teaches us, *"But this kind of demon does not go out except by prayer and fasting."* Ready to overcome your struggles? Click here to learn more about this course.

Embrace the journey ahead with faith, for through prayer, fasting, and the dismantling of evil altars, you shall unlock the doors to spiritual liberation and divine breakthrough. May your path be illuminated by His grace as you walk towards a life free from bondage.

If you're seeing this from the physical copy, type the link: madueke.com/courses in your browser to view all the courses on my website.

Prayer Madueke
CHRISTIAN AUTHOR

Christian Counselling

We were created for a greater purpose than only survival and God wants us to live a full life.

If you need prayer or counselling, or if you have any other inquiries, please visit the counselling page on my website to know when I will be available for a phone call.

Click or type **links.madueke.com/counselling** in your browser.

Let's Connect on Youtube ▶

Join me on my YouTube channel, "Prayer M. Madueke," where I share powerful insights, guidance, and prayers for spiritual breakthroughs.

Subscribe today to unlock the secrets of the Kingdom and embrace an abundant life. Let's grow together!

Click or type **links.madueke.com/youtube** in your browser.

An Invitation to Become a Ministry Partner

I appreciate the support and inquiries I have received regarding collaboration with my ministry. Your prayers and dedication to the work of the Kingdom are highly valued.

You can also visit the donation page on my website if you would like to contribute or learn more about supporting my ministry: madueke.com/donate.

Thank you for your continued support and faithfulness in Christ Jesus.